Using
Google Earth™:

Bring the **World**
into Your Classroom

Level **3-5**

Author

JoBea Holt, Ph.D.

SHELL EDUCATION

The author would like to thank her family for all their support, ideas, and critical reviews.

Publishing Credits

Dona Herweck Rice, *Editor-in-Chief;* Robin Erickson, *Production Director;*
Lee Aucoin, *Creative Director;* Timothy J. Bradley, *Illustration Manager;*
Sara Johnson, M.S. Ed., *Senior Editor;* Hillary Wolfe, *Editor;*
Tracy Edmunds, *Associate Education Editor;* Juan Chavolla, *Cover Designer;*
Corinne Burton, M.A.Ed., *Publisher*

Standards
©2004 Mid-continent Research for Education and Learning (McREL)
©2007 Teachers of English to Speakers of Other Languages, Inc. (TESOL)

Shell Education

5301 Oceanus Drive
Huntington Beach, CA 92649-1030
http://www.tcmpub.com
ISBN 978-1-4258-0825-9
© 2012 Teacher Created Materials, Inc.

Table of Contents

Research and Introduction

No matter how hard you look, you will never find Oz, Neverland, or Narnia on a map. But, if you know where to look and what to look for, you will find the great Mississippi River where Minn and Huck Finn traveled, the prairies and woods where Laura and Caddie grew up, and San Nicolas Island where Karana and Rontu became friends. You may discover that Minn and Huck passed by the starting point for Lewis and Clark's expedition, only at a different time, or that Karana eventually was rescued and taken to the mission in Santa Barbara. Or, you may discover that Laura's family moved from their little house on the prairie because it was in Indian Territory, or that your grandmother lives where Caddie played.

Using Google Earth™: Bring the World into Your Classroom introduces students to Google Earth, and more importantly, to Earth itself. There is so much Earth can tell us about the landscapes where explorers traveled, the settings in classic children's literature, and how the forces of nature shape our planet's surface.

Objectives

There are several objectives for *Using Google Earth™: Bring the World into Your Classroom*:

1. To introduce students to children's literature, social studies, mathematics, and Earth science through a very visual experience.

2. To add an exciting geographic dimension to reading, social studies, mathematics, and science.

3. To create student-generated maps that link students' personal worlds to the worlds of literature, science, mathematics, and social studies.

4. To allow students to build a Google Earth™ folder system to record where they travel in their reading adventures, social studies lessons, and in their personal experiences.

5. To encourage project-based learning and authentic tasks.

6. To align with national standards in social studies, science, mathematics, language arts, geography, and technology.

"Geography is an integrating discipline that helps students understand, participate in, and make informed decisions about the world around them" (Shultz et al. 2008). By using images of Earth as an integrating force, literature, social studies, mathematics, and science flow together. "The interactive nature of virtual globes can facilitate learning through an enjoyable and individually-oriented session..." (Shultz et al. 2008). The ability to use a three-dimensional model of Earth facilitates understanding of the Earth system and the many subject areas that it comprises, from science, to history, to art, or any topic with a geographic component (SERC 2009). Plus, research suggests that when technology is integrated throughout the curriculum, students will not only learn technology skills but also content (Silverstein et al. 2000).

Research and Introduction *(cont.)*

Teaching with Technology

Using Google Earth encourages the teacher to step out of a traditional lecture-based mode of teaching and into the role of facilitator or coach as students navigate through the program. Cognitive research shows that learning improves when students are actively involved in learning, working in groups, frequently interacting and receiving feedback, and seeing the connections to real life (Roschelle et al. 2001). One goal of this resource is to show students (and teachers) that this technology is more than just a fun tool—it provides an access point for content-area instruction. "It is important to remember that teaching students how to use the program is not enough. Think about why the students are using the program. What project can they accomplish? What question or problem can they solve when they use the program to create a product?" (Frei, Gammill, and Irons 2007). *Using Google Earth™: Bring the World into Your Classroom* offers students an entry way into the curriculum that is broad, authentic, and engaging. And the more students practice functioning in creative, integrated, collaborative learning domains across all the content areas, the better (Bean 2010).

Because Google Earth is inherently engaging and maneuverable, it is a natural fit for interactive whiteboards and computer use in classrooms. Students will learn to see Earth in new ways and to explore and develop stories about what they discover. According to the Project New Media Literacies (Card, Mackinlay, and Shneiderman 1999), maps offer students opportunities for visualization, and better visualization makes us smarter. "Google Maps/Earth are helping us tell stories better and bringing geographic data to life in ways that make traditional maps look more like decorations on the wall" (Castiglione 2009). With this resource, students can build a growing set of maps that record their adventures in books and in class, and tie these adventures to their family histories and personal experiences.

Google Earth and Reading

Through Google Earth, teachers can also incorporate informational text into their lessons from sources such as *TIME® for Kids*, NASA's *Earth Observatory* website, and *National Geographic* magazine. Reading informational text is a key initiative from the Common Core Curriculum Standards for Language Arts, especially in terms of analyzing key ideas and details, and the integration of knowledge and ideas (Common Core State Standards 2010). By tying informational text to a real-world setting, and then having students experience that location in an authentic visual way, they are able to add dimension to the details described in the text, as well as build schema as they integrate new information into their existing understanding of the world.

Overview of Google Earth

Images from Space

The first picture of Earth was not inspiring. It was taken in 1946 by a 35mm camera on a V-2 missile at an altitude of 65 miles and was very fuzzy. Perhaps the most important image of Earth taken by the National Aeronautics and Space Administration (NASA) is called Earthrise—an image captured in 1968 on Apollo 8, the first manned mission to orbit the Moon, by astronaut Bill Anders. He said, "We came all this way to explore the Moon, and the most important thing is that we discovered the Earth." The first Earth Day soon followed.

NASA continues to take images of Earth, but now focuses on using a variety of instruments operating at a wide range of wavelengths in order to measure our atmosphere, land surface, and oceans.

A suite of NASA satellites continuously monitors key factors that help scientists understand our water, energy, and biological cycles. To see these datasets in detail, visit http://earthobservatory.nasa.gov/GlobalMaps/.

IMAGE COURTESY OF NASA'S ASTRONOMY PICTURE OF THE DAY WEBSITE: HTTP:// ANTWRP.AGEGSFC.NASA.GOV/APOD/AP101115. HTML

Astronaut Tracy Caldwell Dyson enjoys the view from the International Space Station's window

However, ask any astronaut what they spend their spare time doing in orbit, and most will say they spend it looking out the window of the Space Shuttle or the International Space Station, watching Earth go by. Their photographs are one of their most valued treasures from their missions, and all are available for us to see. Visit the Gateway to Astronaut Photography of Earth's website at http://eol.jsc.nasa.gov/. The best and most relevant images are presented on NASA's Earth Observatory (http://earthobservatory.nasa.gov/), a website that keeps us informed of dynamic and timely events with daily images of Earth.

IMAGE COURTESY OF NASA'S ASTRONOMY PICTURE OF THE DAY WEBSITE: HTTP://APOD.NASA.GOV/APOD/AP081224.HTML

"Earthrise" photograph from Apollo 8, the first manned mission to orbit the moon

Overview of Google Earth *(cont.)*

What Is Google Earth ?

Google Earth is both a data set and a software tool.

Data Set

The data set consists of thousands of high-resolution images of our planet taken from space that have been mosaicked together onto a globe. The global mosaic primarily contains cloud-free images of the highest resolution. In some cases, however, nearby images can look quite different if they have been taken in a different season, at a different time of day, or with a different instrument.

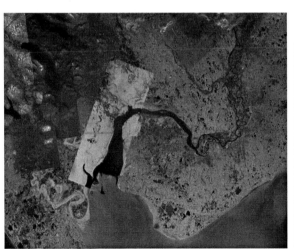

IMAGE ©2010 TERRAMETRICS, ©2010 GOOGLE, DATA SIO, NOAA, U.S. NAVY, NGA, GEBCO, ©2010 EUROPA TECHNOLOGIES

A view of southern Alaska showing images from a variety of seasons, sun angles, and instruments.

Images from past times, going back to the 1940s, can also be accessed using Google Earth in some locations. Some of these are black and white and many are of much lower resolution than the latest versions, but all can tell us something about how our planet has changed. Many of the Google Earth images have been taken by NASA instruments on satellites in polar orbits.

Software Tool

The second part of Google Earth is the software that allows users to explore the mosiacked images. This software operates through the Internet to allow a user to "fly" to any place on Earth at almost any resolution without keeping a high-resolution global data set on his or her computer.

In 2010, NASA flew an instrument called Shuttle Radar Topography Mission (SRTM) on the Space Shuttle. The instrument used two imaging radar antennas configured to measure the topography of the entire land surface between the latitudes of 60° north and south in only 11 days. This digital topographic data set has been layered on top of the Google Earth image globe to provide Google Earth 's 3D capabilities.

Most recently, several organizations, including the U.S. Navy and the National Oceanic and Atmospheric Administration (NOAA), have provided ocean data to Google Earth. This capability is rapidly being enhanced to allow users to explore beneath the surface of the sea.

How to Use This Book

Using Google Earth™: Bring the World in Your Classroom was created by a former NASA scientist to provide teachers with a manageable way to access this technology in the context of content-area lessons, and use the features in the images to teach students about the history and sciences of our planet. Each lesson introduces and demonstrates one or more Google Earth tools within a simple, easy-to-follow format, always keeping the standard as the focus of the lesson.

The first three units of this resource introduce students to the basic features of Google Earth. The first unit introduces students to the Earth in the **3D viewer**, the **navigation tools**, and the **Search**, **Places**, and **Layers panels**. The lessons are organized to build student competency with Google Earth. The second unit teaches students how to see natural, artificial, and abstract features on Earth and provides a means of referencing the scale of features they are seeing. The third unit shows students how to save and organize the places they visit so that these places can be compared to places students visit in the future.

In the remaining five units, students will learn to explore our planet in Google Earth in the context of content-area lessons, including language arts, social studies, science, and mathematics, as well as a cross-curricular unit that includes space exploration, the oceans, art, and imaginary places.

The information on pages 8–12 outlines the major components and purposes for each activity and pages 14–21 detail how to prepare for instruction. Page 13 gives a visual reference of the main Google Earth tools used in this book.

How to Use This Book *(cont.)*

Lesson Plan

Standard shows the geography objective addressed in the activity. Content-area lessons address the subject-specific standard in addition to geography.

Google Earth Tools are listed here. Tools introduced in the lesson are denoted with an asterisk. Use the *Google Earth Reference Window* on page 13 and the Teacher Resource CD (Reference.pdf) to familiarize yourself with the locations of the various tools.

Vocabulary words and **Materials** are shown here.

Procedure, a step-by-step description of the lesson, is shown here. It is recommended that teachers work through the procedure for each lesson in Google Earth and preset all placemarks before presenting the lesson to students.

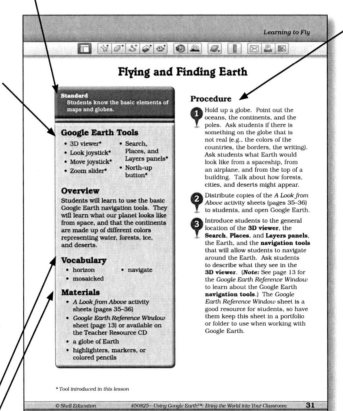

How to Use This Book *(cont.)*

Lesson Plan *(cont.)*

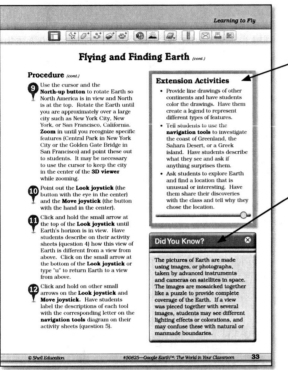

Extension Activities provide opportunities for independent practice, or allow teachers to add more dimension or provide additional challenges.

Did You Know? offers related information and fun facts to help students make connections across content areas and activate their prior knowledge.

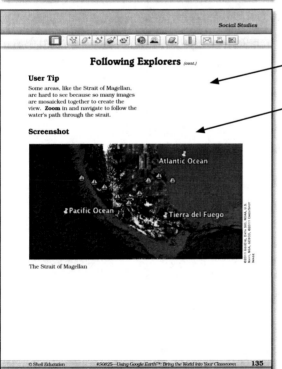

User Tips offer technical advice or shortcuts.

Screenshots provide a visual frame of reference.

How to Use This Book *(cont.)*

Lesson Plan *(cont.)*

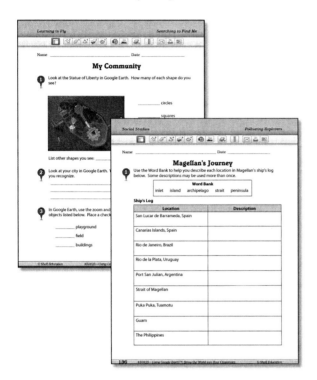

Student Activity Sheets assess students' content knowledge as well as their Google Earth technology skills. Answer keys are provided in Appendix B (pages 224–229), and an Assessment Rubric Guide is available in Appendix C (pages 230–231), and on the Teacher Resource CD (Tech_Rubric.pdf).

The **Teacher Resource CD** contains reproducible copies of all the student activity pages and additional teacher resources. See Appendix H for a list of CD contents.

How to Use This Book *(cont.)*

Preparing for Lessons

Before presenting each lesson, work through the lesson yourself in Google Earth and **placemark** each location. Then, when you are presenting to the class, you can double-click on each **placemark** in the **Places panel** to fly directly to each location.

Google Earth Reference Window

Distribute copies of the **Google Earth Reference Window** to students at the beginning of the first lesson. Make a copy for yourself as well or enlarge it and display it in the classroom. This visual reference will be very helpful in identifying **Google Earth Tools** as you work through the lessons.

Lesson Presentation

The **Procedures** in each lesson describe how to manipulate Google Earth on a projected screen or interactive whiteboard in front of students. Students can observe Google Earth on the screen or whiteboard and fill out their activity sheets.

Depending on your classroom setup, there are a number of alternative ways to present the lessons:

• Ask individual students to manipulate Google Earth using the class computer or interactive whiteboard during the lessons.

• If students have their own computers or small groups of students can share computers, they can follow along through each step of the lesson.

• Present part of the lesson to students as a group and then let them complete the activity sheets using their computers.

The **Extension Activities** are designed to be completed by individual students or small groups of students after they have received instruction in the main lesson.

Google Earth Reference Window

Toolbar

Placemark · Polygon · Path · Image Overlay · Tour · Clock · Sun · Planets · Ruler · Email · Print · View in Google Maps™

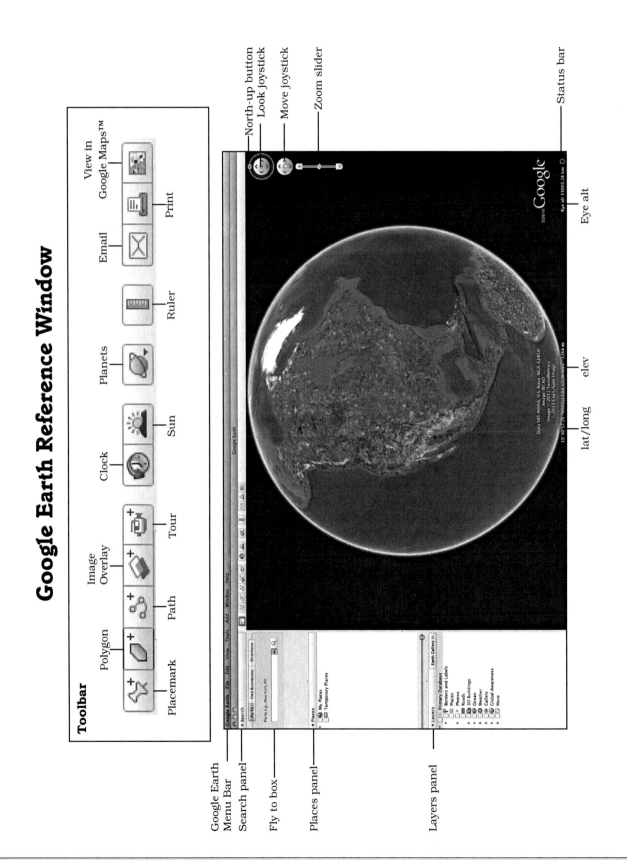

North-up button
Look joystick
Move joystick
Zoom slider
Status bar

Google Earth
Menu Bar
Search panel
Fly to box
Places panel
Layers panel

Eye alt
elev
lat/long

Preparing for Google Earth Instruction *(cont.)*

Preparing the Technology

Exploring with Google Earth requires a computer, access to the Internet (preferably through a direct line connection), and display technology in your classroom.

1. System Requirements

Google Earth runs on both PCs and Macs. System requirements to run Google Earth 6.0 for Macs and PCs and video card requirements are shown here:

System Requirements

PC	Mac
Minimum:	**Minimum:**
• Operating System: Windows XP, Windows Vista, or Windows 7 • CPU: Pentium 3, 500Mhz • System Memory (RAM): 256 MB • Hard Disk: 400MB free space • Screen: 1024 × 768, "16-bit High Color" DirectX9 (to run in Direct X mode) • Graphics Card: Direct X9 and 3D capable with 64 MB of VRAM • Network speed: 128 Kbits/sec	• Operating System: Mac OS X 10.5.0 or later • CPU: Any Intel Mac • System Memory (RAM): 256 MB • Hard Disk: 400MB free space • Screen: 1024 × 768, "Thousands of Colors" • Graphics Card: Direct X9 and 3D capable with 64 MB of VRAM • Network speed: 128 Kbits/sec
Recommended:	**Recommended:**
• Operating System: Windows XP, Windows Vista, or Windows 7 • CPU: Pentium 4, 2.4GHz+ or AMD 2400xp+ • System Memory (RAM): 512 MB • Hard Disk: 2GB free space • Screen: 1280 × 1024, "32-bit True Color" • Graphics Card: Direct X9 and 3D capable with 256 MB of VRAM • Network speed: 768 Kbits/sec	• Operating System: Mac OS X 10.5.2 or later • CPU: Dual Core Intel Mac • System Memory (RAM): 512 MB • Hard Disk: 2GB free space • Screen: 1280 × 1024, "Millions of Colors" • Graphics Card: Direct X9 and 3D capable with 256 MB of VRAM • Network speed: 768 Kbits/sec

Note: A version of Google Earth is available for the iPad™, but it does not include many of the features used in these lessons.

Preparing for Google Earth Instruction *(cont.)*

Preparing the Technology *(cont.)*

2. **Internet Requirements**

   High-speed Internet is required to run Google Earth. The minimum speed required is 128 Kbits/sec and the recommended speed is a minimum of 768 Kbits/sec.

   Google Earth requires a large amount of bandwidth to run. If you are using a wireless connection, the screen may freeze and Google Earth will need to be restarted. If the problem persists, try connecting directly to your router via an ethernet cable. Full resolution views of the most recent places you visited are saved temporarily on your computer's cache, and can be replayed from the hard drive without connecting to the Internet.

   Some school sites use Internet blockers or firewalls which can interfere with Google Earth content.

3. **Display Technology for Flexible Grouping**

   The optimum means to display Google Earth is to use an interactive whiteboard or a projector with your computer. Students may interact with the program by coming up to the board or by pressing the appropriate keys on the teacher's computer keyboard. Alternately, small groups of students may gather around a single computer and work through the lessons together. If you are using this resource in a lab where students each have access to a computer, students may observe as the teacher introduces the lesson, and then continue to work through the lesson at their own stations.

4. **Maintaining Student and Classroom .kmz Files**

   Students have the opportunity to develop files that record their adventures in the Google Earth file format called Keyhole Markup Language (**.kml**). Most files in Google Earth use the extension **.kmz**, which stands for KML-zipped. Ideally, students will maintain these **.kmz files** throughout their school careers. Given that students may do some of their work on school computers and some on home computers, students may choose to keep their working **.kmz files** on a memory stick. Instruct students on how to also maintain a backup file on their home or classroom computer in case the memory stick is lost. Ensure students save their entire **.kmz file** at the end of the school year so that it is ready to augment the following year.

Preparing for Google Earth Instruction *(cont.)*

Setting Up Google Earth

Google Earth is a program that can be downloaded from the Internet for free. To use the program, you must have access to the Internet with the specifications outlined on page 14.

1. Download Google Earth

Open your Internet browser, go to http://earth.google.com, click on "Download Google Earth," and then "Agree and Download." Look for the .dmg file on your desktop or in your download folder (Mac) or the .exe file (PC) and click on it to install it. Follow the directions for installing Google Earth on your computer. If you use a Mac, find Google Earth in your **Applications** folder and drag it to your dock. If you use a PC, find Google Earth in your **Programs** file and create a shortcut on your desktop.

Open Google Earth by double-clicking on the Google Earth icon in your dock or desktop. *Note:* If the "Tip" window opens, click the button that says you no longer want this window and close it. You will see the **3D viewer** (a picture of Earth with the sky in the background) on the right, and three panels titled **Search**, **Places**, and **Layers** on the left. You are now ready to explore!

Note: Keep a copy of the *Google Earth Reference Window* near your keyboard as you begin to explore in Google Earth. Give each student a copy to use as they learn new tools, or enlarge the *Google Earth Reference Window* and post it where it will be visible to all and easily referenced during lessons.

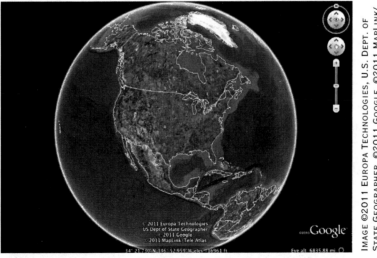

3D viewer in Google Earth

Preparing for Google Earth Instruction *(cont.)*

Setting Up Google Earth *(cont.)*

2. Set Your Preferences

To access the **Preferences** settings on a Mac, click on **Google Earth** in the **Google Earth Menu Bar**, and choose **Preferences** from the dropdown menu. On a PC, click on **Tools**, then **Options**, and choose **Google Earth Options** from the dropdown menu to open the **Preferences window**. Set your Google Earth preferences to match the screenshots that follow.

Choose "Feet, Miles" or "Meters, Kilometers"

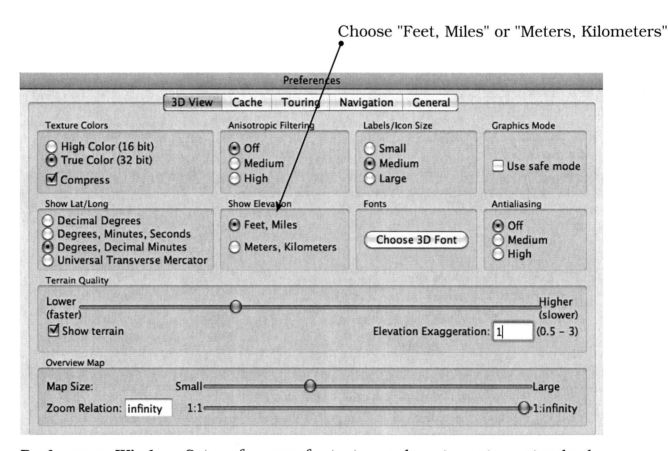

Preferences Window: Set preferences for texture colors, icon sizes, standard or metric measurements, fonts, terrain quality, and map size.

Preparing for Google Earth Instruction *(cont.)*

Setting Up Google Earth *(cont.)*

2. Set Your Preferences *(cont.)*

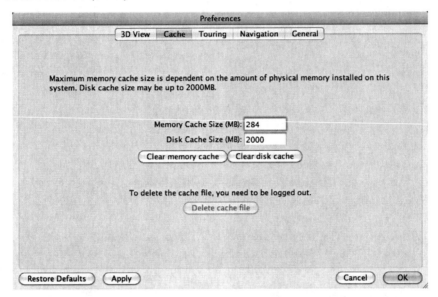

Cache tab: You can make the cache size as large as 2,000 MB (2 Gigabytes). By having a large cache, you can save your latest Google Earth views and find them even without Internet access.

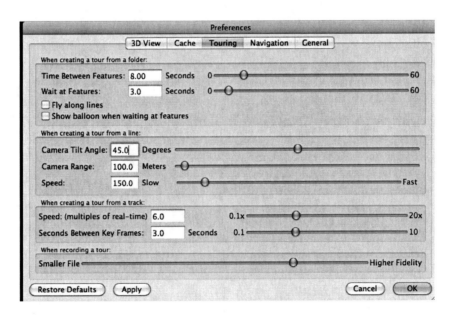

Touring tab: Adjust the settings for touring. Try to keep the speeds low enough so students can keep track of where they are going.

Preparing for Google Earth Instruction *(cont.)*

Setting Up Google Earth *(cont.)*
2. Set Your Preferences *(cont.)*

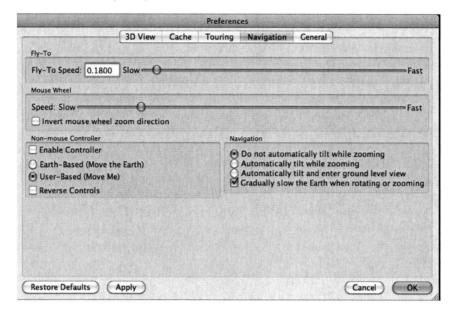

Navigation tab: Change settings for "flying" speeds and set preferences for tilt and ground level views.

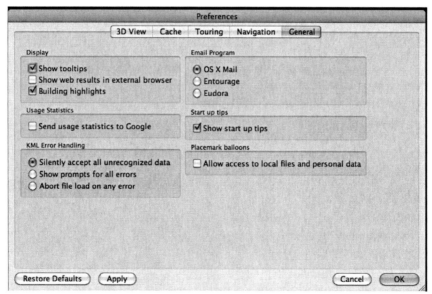

General tab: Set your display preferences and choose the appropriate email program you wish to access for sending files. Select whether to see user tips every time Google Earth starts, and allow your **placemarks** compatibility with other files and data.

Preparing for Google Earth Instruction *(cont.)*

Setting Up Google Earth *(cont.)*

3. Set the View Menu

In the **Google Earth Menu Bar** across the top of the screen, click on **View** and turn on the following options:

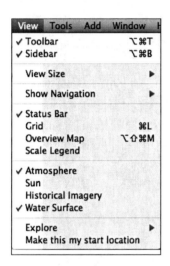

4. Select the Fly To Tab

In the **Search panel,** select the **Fly To tab** (instead of the **Find Businesses tab** or the **Directions tab**).

5. Turn Off Folders and Layers

Before starting each lesson, be sure all layers in the **Layers panel** are turned off, except perhaps the **Borders and Labels layer**. Look through your **Places panel** and turn off any **placemarks** that are not relevant to your lesson. Or, leave the **placemarks** turned on to compare places your class has visited.

6. Apply Google SafeSearch™

Make sure that Google SafeSearch is set to *strict filtering* as Google Earth will provide students with access to the Internet. Open the Google home page (http://www.google.com/) and look in the upper right corner for the **gear icon**. Click the **gear icon** and select *Search Settings*. Look for *SafeSearch Filtering* and select *Use strict filtering (Filter both explicit text and explicit images)*. Then, click **Save Preferences** to save.

Preparing for Google Earth Instruction *(cont.)*

Important Technology Notes

Using the Mouse

Lesson procedures often call for right-clicking with the mouse. If you have a single-click mouse or a trackpad, you can use control-click to accomplish the same function.

Finding Locations

Some locations may be tricky to find in Google Earth. Before using the **Fly to box** to search for a specific location, first navigate to the general area of the Earth. Always preview each location before presenting a lesson to students.

Printing

Images from Google Earth should be printed at a high resolution, but color printing can be expensive. Consider saving images as PDFs and displaying your images onscreen rather than printing them.

Updating Google Earth

Like any evolving technology, Google Earth is constantly updating their application and services. Always make sure you have the most up-to-date version downloaded, and install updates regularly. Depending on the version you use, tools and commands may be found in slightly different locations on the screen than what is described in this resource.

Google Earth is contantly updating the layers data. If any of the layers used in these lessons do not appear in the **Layers panel**, search in the **Google Earth Gallery** for the missing layers.

Getting Help

The How-to Guide in Appendix D of this book (pages 232-238) contains instructions for using most Google Earth tools. For additional help, see the online Google Earth Support pages (http://earth.google.com/support). Google Earth is fairly intuitive, and in most cases, the online resource will be able to help you solve your problem.

Differentiation

Why Differentiate?

To successfully differentiate instruction, teachers must first know their students. Teachers must determine the readiness levels of students, as well as take into consideration the type of support they may need. It is important to make adjustments in the curriculum when students are having trouble with the material. Finding new ways to present information, using manipulatives or realia, and providing opportunities for targeted support are important aspects of a differentiated classroom.

Below are some reasons why and ways to differentiate the curriculum for diverse learners using this resource.

- **Content:** Vary the content (what is being taught or the materials students will use) when students are not at the same academic readiness level.
- **Process:** Vary the process (how it is taught or what amount of support you provide students) when you have students with diverse learning styles or readiness levels.
- **Product:** Vary the product (what students produce) when you have students with a variety of different readiness levels, interests, and passions.

Using *Google Earth™: The World in Your Classroom* offers a tremendous opportunity for differentiation with an authentic and engaging way to capture student interest and have them connect to the material. The interactive nature of Google Earth requires students to engage in higher-order thinking skills as they analyze what they see, apply their knowledge of locations to new settings, synthesize the information they discover, and evaluate the effects of social and environmental conditions on geography. This is an inherent differentiation strategy built into the lessons because all students will approach these tasks and questions at their own readiness and ability levels.

Content

When using this resource with below-level learners and English language learners, key vocabulary terms are called out so that they may be introduced before each activity. Provide graphic organizers or word banks to scaffold instruction. In addition, each lesson offers an **Extension Activity** for above-level learners. Use these activities to encourage more in-depth investigation of a topic or to ask students to apply the skills they have learned in an alternate setting or situation.

Differentiation *(cont.)*

Why Differentiate? *(cont.)*

Process

The lessons in *Google Earth™: The World in Your Classroom* offer students the ability to participate in authentic tasks with real-world applications. By exploring and investigating Earth, students are actively engaged in discovery learning, inquiry-based learning, and authentic problem-solving. Students can work in flexible group arrangements, with partners, in small groups, or individually. The **Extension Activities** suggest ideas for students to complete independent investigations, and can be modified for below-level students or English language learners to be completed in pairs or small groups. The lessons can be slowed down or sped up depending on the readiness levels of the students, as well.

Product

The activities in *Google Earth™: The World in Your Classroom* appeal to students' varying interests. Students draw, write, and research. They build models, interact with technology, and use kinesthetic methods to experience and retain information. Tier the products in the lessons and assign appropriate products to match student readiness levels. Allow above-level students to extend their learning by creating more challenging products as a result of the lessons. For example, students can create visual art based on what they saw in Google Earth, or create and narrate an interactive presentation.

Additional Differentiation Strategies

The research-based strategies above can be used to differentiate the content, process, and product (Conklin 2011) of this resource. The next section offers a brief definition of each strategy.

Differentiation (cont.)

Strategies for Working with English Language Learners

Google Earth offers a truly visual and experiential way to see Earth, investigate science, uncover mathematical concepts, participate in history, and become immersed in literature—a practical resource for diverse learning styles. For English language learners, this tool provides incredible support and access to the curriculum.

Nevertheless, it is appropriate to provide additional scaffolds to these learners. Here are some ways to support the English language learners in your classroom.

1. **Use visual media as an alternative to written responses.**

   The activities in this book offer options for students to sketch or capture screenshots or use pictures in their answers.

2. **Frame questions to make language accessible.**

   When possible, provide word banks and introduce key vocabulary before completing the activities. This will help students use new words in context. Sentence frames or question frames can also make the language more accessible. Some examples include:

   - Would it be better if...?
   - How is_____ related to _____?
   - Why is _____ important?
   - Why is _____ better than _____?

3. **Give context to questions to enable understanding.**

   Use pictures and icons to help students recall key instructions and vocabulary. The activities in this book include **screenshots** to help provide visual references, and the icons are highlighted as well.

4. **Provide sentence frames or stems to encourage higher-order thinking.**

   Providing language tools will help students express what they think and will help you get the information you are looking for. In addition, these frames will provide models for oral language responses. Some examples include:

   - This is important because...
   - This is better because...
   - This is similar to...
   - This is different from...
   - I agree/disagree with _____ because...
   - I think _____ because...

Standards Correlations

Shell Education is committed to producing educational materials that are research- and standards-based. In this effort, we have correlated all of our products to the academic standards of all 50 United States, the District of Columbia, the Department of Defense Dependent Schools, and all Canadian provinces. We have also correlated to the Common Core State Standards.

How to Find Standards Correlations

To print a customized correlation report of this product for your state, visit our website at http://www.shelleducation. com and follow the on-screen directions. If you require assistance in printing correlation reports, please contact Customer Service at 1-877-777-3450.

Purpose and Intent of Standards

Legislation mandates that all states adopt academic standards that identify the skills students will learn in kindergarten through grade twelve. Many states also have standards for Pre-K. This same legislation sets requirements to ensure the standards are detailed and comprehensive.

Standards are designed to focus instruction and guide adoption of curricula. Standards are statements that describe the criteria necessary for students to meet specific academic goals. They define the knowledge, skills, and content students should acquire at each level. Standards are also used to develop standardized tests to evaluate students' academic progress. Teachers are required to demonstrate how their lessons meet state standards. State standards are used in the development of all of our products, so educators can be assured they meet the academic requirements of each state.

McREL Compendium

We use the Mid-continent Research for Education and Learning (McREL) Compendium to create standards correlations. Each year, McREL analyzes state standards and revises the compendium. By following this procedure, McREL is able to produce a general compilation of national standards. Each lesson in this product is based on one or more McREL standards. The chart on pages 26-29 lists each standard taught in this product and the page number(s) for the corresponding lesson(s).

TESOL Standards

The lessons in this book promote English language development for English language learners. The standards listed on page 30 support the language objectives presented throughout the lessons.

Standards Correlations *(cont.)*

Lesson Title	Standard
Flying and Finding Earth (pages 31–36)	Geography: Students know the basic elements of maps and globes.
Searching to Find Me (pages 37–42)	Geography: Students know major physical and human features of places as they are represented on maps and globes.
Saving Your Place (pages 43–48)	Geography: Students know how the characteristics of places are shaped by physical and human processes.
Exploring with Layers (pages 49–54)	Geography: Students know that physical systems affect human systems.
Identifying Artificial Features (pages 55–60)	Geography: Students understand how physical processes help to shape features and patterns on Earth's surface.
Investigating Natural Features (pages 61–66)	Geography: Students know the physical processes that shape patterns on Earth's surface.
Overlaying Abstract Features (pages 67–72)	Geography: Students use map grids (e.g., latitude and longitude or alphanumeric system) to plot absolute location.
Creating Reference Scales (pages 73–78)	Geography: Students understand the spatial organization of places through such concepts as location, distance, direction, scale, movement, and region.
Sorting Our Folders (pages 79–84)	Geography: Students understand the characteristics and uses of maps, globes, and other geographic tools and technologies.
Following Our Family Trees (pages 85–90)	Geography: Students understand the nature and complexity of Earth's cultural mosaics.
Making Literature Connections (pages 91–96)	Geography: Students know how differences in perception affect people's interpretations of the world.
Building History Connections (pages 97–102)	Geography: Students understand how geography is used to interpret the past.
Mapping the Plot of a Book (pages 103–108)	Geography: Students understand how physical systems affect human systems. Language Arts: Students understand elements of character development in literary works.

Standards Correlations *(cont.)*

Lesson Title	Standard
Following the Path of a Book (pages 109–114)	Geography: Students know the ways in which changes in people's perceptions of environments have influenced human migration and settlement over time. Language Arts: Students make, confirm, and revise simple predictions about what will be found in a text.
Touring a Book (pages 115–120)	Geography: Students know the ways in which changes in people's perceptions of environments have influenced human migration and settlement over time. Language Arts: Students summarize and paraphrase information in texts.
Creating a Book Report (pages 121–126)	Geography: Students know the ways in which changes in people's perceptions of environments have influenced human migration and settlement over time. Language Arts: Students make basic oral presentations to class.
Going Back in Time (pages 127–132)	Geography: Students know the ways people alter the physical environment. History: Students know about life in urban areas and communities of various cultures of the world at various times in their history.
Following Explorers (pages 133–138)	Geography: Students know the geographic factors that have influenced people and events in the past. World History: Students know about European explorers of the 15th and 16th centuries, their reasons for exploring, the information gained from their journeys, and what happened as a result of their travels.
Mapping History (pages 139–144)	Geography: Students know the factors that have contributed to changing land use in a community. History: Students understand the people, events, problems, and ideas that were significant in creating the history of their state.

Standards Correlations *(cont.)*

Lesson Title	Standard
Tracking the News (pages 145–150)	Geography: Students know natural hazards that occur in the physical environment.
	Historical Understanding: Students know how to interpret data presented in timelines (e.g., identify the time at which events occurred; the sequence in which events developed; what else was occurring at the time).
Understanding the Water Cycle (pages 151–156)	Geography: Students understand the characteristics of ecosystems on Earth's surface.
	Science: Students understand atmospheric processes and the water cycle.
Discovering Forces of Change (pages 157–162)	Geography: Students know the physical processes that shape patterns on Earth's surface.
	Science: Students know how features on Earth's surface are constantly changed by a combination of slow and rapid processes.
Shading the Earth (pages 163–168)	Geography: Students know how Earth's position relative to the Sun affects events and conditions on Earth.
	Science: Students know that the Sun provides the light and heat necessary to maintain the temperature of Earth.
Using Energy (pages 169–174)	Geography: Students know the relationships between economic activities and resources.
	Science: Students know the sources and properties of energy.
Building a Capital (pages 175–180)	Geography: Students understand the spatial organization of places through such concepts as location, distance, direction, scale, movement, and region.
	Mathematics: Students understand and apply basic and advanced properties of the concepts of geometry.

Standards Correlations *(cont.)*

Lesson Title	Standard
Estimating Deforestation (pages 181–186)	Geography: Students know ways in which humans can change ecosystems. Mathematics: Students use specific strategies to estimate quantities and measurements.
Measuring America (pages 187–192)	Geography: Students know the characteristics and locations of cities and how cities have changed over time. Mathematics: Students understand and apply basic and advanced properties of the concepts of measurement.
Designing Crops (pages 193–198)	Geography: Students know how human activities have increased the ability of the physical environment to support human life in the local community, state, United States, and other countries. Mathematics: Students understand the basic measures of perimeter, area, volume, capacity, mass, angle, and circumference.
Exploring Space (pages 199–204)	Science: Students know that astronomical objects in space are massive in size and are separated from one another by vast distances. United States History: Students understand the impact of postwar scientific research on contemporary society (e.g., the U.S. space program).
Diving Into the Ocean (pages 205–210)	Geography: Students know the physical components of Earth's atmosphere, lithosphere, hydrosphere, and biosphere. Students understand ways in which human action has contributed to long-term changes in the natural environments in particular regions or worldwide.
Imagining Places (pages 211–216)	Geography: Students understand similarities and differences within and among literary works from various genres and cultures. Language Arts: Students know that film and television have features that identify different genres.
Drawing on Earth (pages 217–222)	Art: Students understand connections among the various art forms and other disciplines.

Standards Correlations *(cont.)*

TESOL Standards

Lesson	Content Area	Standard
All lessons	All content areas	To use English to communicate in social settings: Students will use English to participate in social interactions.
All lessons	All content areas	To use English to communicate in social settings: Students will interact in, through, and with spoken and written English for personal expression and enjoyment.
All lessons	All content areas	To use English to communicate in social settings: Students will use learning strategies to extend their communicative competence.
All lessons	All content areas	To use English to achieve academically in all content areas: Students will use English to interact in the classroom.
All lessons	All content areas	To use English to achieve academically in all content areas: Students will use English to obtain, process, construct, and provide subject matter information in spoken and written form.
All lessons	All content areas	To use English to achieve academically in all content areas: Students will use appropriate learning strategies to construct and apply academic knowledge.
All lessons	All content areas	To use English in socially and culturally appropriate ways: Students will use the appropriate language variety, register, and genre according to audience, purpose, and setting.
All lessons	All content areas	To use English in socially and culturally appropriate ways: Students will use nonverbal communication appropriate to audience, purpose, and setting.
All lessons	All content areas	To use English in socially and culturally appropriate ways: Students will use appropriate learning strategies to extend their sociolinguistic and sociocultural competence.

Flying and Finding Earth

Standard
Students know the basic elements of maps and globes.

Google Earth Tools

- 3D viewer*
- Look joystick*
- Move joystick*
- Zoom slider*
- Search, Places, and Layers panels*
- North-up button*

Overview

Students will learn to use the basic Google Earth navigation tools. They will learn what our planet looks like from space, and that the continents are made up of different colors representing water, forests, ice, and deserts.

Vocabulary

- horizon
- mosaicked
- navigate

Materials

- *A Look from Above* activity sheets (pages 35–36)
- *Google Earth Reference Window* sheet (page 13) or available on the Teacher Resource CD
- a globe of Earth
- highlighters, markers, or colored pencils

Procedure

1. Hold up a globe. Point out the oceans, the continents, and the poles. Ask students if there is something on the globe that is not real (e.g., the colors of the countries, the borders, the writing). Ask students what Earth would look like from a spaceship, from an airplane, and from the top of a building. Talk about how forests, cities, and deserts might appear.

2. Distribute copies of the *A Look from Above* activity sheets (pages 35–36) to students, and open Google Earth.

3. Introduce students to the general location of the **3D viewer**, the **Search**, **Places**, and **Layers panels**, the Earth, and the **navigation tools** that will allow students to navigate around the Earth. Ask students to describe what they see in the **3D viewer**. (**Note:** See page 13 for the *Google Earth Reference Window* to learn about the Google Earth **navigation tools**.) The *Google Earth Reference Window* sheet is a good resource for students, so have them keep this sheet in a portfolio or folder to use when working with Google Earth.

* Tool introduced in this lesson

Flying and Finding Earth *(cont.)*

Procedure *(cont.)*

4 Place the cursor over Earth in the **3D viewer** and click, hold, and drag with your mouse to rotate Earth. Look for an ocean, a desert (e.g., the Sahara), a forest (e.g., the Amazon, the Congo), an island (e.g., Cuba, Japan), and an ice-and snow-covered region (e.g., Antarctica, Greenland). Ask students to describe each region on their activity sheets (question 1), using three adjectives—one related to color, one related to shape or texture, and one related to their feelings or impressions about the feature. Encourage students to choose words that are more specific than just *beautiful*, *amazing*, or *cool*. Use specific words such as *rust-red* or *goldenrod* for color, *rippled* or *organized* for texture or shape, and *curious* or *cold* for feelings or impressions.

5 Move the Earth using the cursor, and show students that North can be anywhere in the **3D viewer**. Most people are more comfortable seeing North at the top of the Earth. Show students the **North-up button** in the upper-right corner of the **3D viewer**. As you turn Earth with your cursor, the N on the **North-up button** rotates as well.

6 Show students how to use the **Look joystick** and **North-up button** to rotate Earth. First, click on the circular dial that encircles the **North-up button** to "grab" it and drag it clockwise or counter-clockwise. Next, click and hold on one of the directional arrows on the **Look joystick**. Clicking the letter N on the dial encircling the **North-up button** once will return North to the top of the viewer.

7 Use the cursor to move Africa into full view with North at the top of the Earth. On the map on their activity sheets, direct students to color Africa using the colors as they appear on the Google Earth globe (question 2). Ask them to label a desert, an island, a forest, and an ocean. Have students describe what the colors tell them about the features (question 3).

8 Point to the **zoom slider**. Show students how the **+zoom** moves the view closer, and the **-zoom** moves the view further away. **Zoom** in and out to illustrate a good standard elevation for viewing, and a speed of zooming that is acceptable.

Flying and Finding Earth *(cont.)*

Procedure *(cont.)*

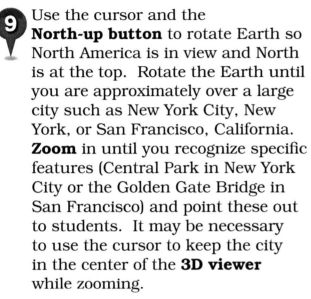

9 Use the cursor and the **North-up button** to rotate Earth so North America is in view and North is at the top. Rotate the Earth until you are approximately over a large city such as New York City, New York, or San Francisco, California. **Zoom** in until you recognize specific features (Central Park in New York City or the Golden Gate Bridge in San Francisco) and point these out to students. It may be necessary to use the cursor to keep the city in the center of the **3D viewer** while zooming.

10 Point out the **Look joystick** (the button with the eye in the center) and the **Move joystick** (the button with the hand in the center).

11 Click and hold the small arrow at the top of the **Look joystick** until Earth's horizon is in view. Have students describe on their activity sheets (question 4) how this view of Earth is different from a view from above. Click on the small arrow at the bottom of the **Look joystick** or type "u" to return Earth to a view from above.

12 Click and hold on other small arrows on the **Look joystick** and **Move joystick.** Have students label the descriptions of each tool with the corresponding letter on the **navigation tools** diagram on their activity sheets (question 5).

Extension Activities

- Provide line drawings of other continents and have students color the drawings. Have them create a legend to represent different types of features.

- Tell students to use the **navigation tools** to investigate the coast of Greenland, the Sahara Desert, or a Greek island. Have students describe what they see and ask if anything surprises them.

- Ask students to explore Earth and find a location that is unusual or interesting. Have them share their discoveries with the class and tell why they chose the location.

Did You Know? ⊗

The pictures of Earth are made using images, or photographs, taken by advanced instruments and cameras on satellites in space. The images are mosaicked together like a puzzle to provide complete coverage of the Earth. If a view was pieced together with several images, students may see different lighting effects or colorations, and may confuse these with natural or manmade boundaries.

Flying and Finding Earth *(cont.)*

Screenshots

North-up button and

Look joystick

Move joystick

Zoom slider

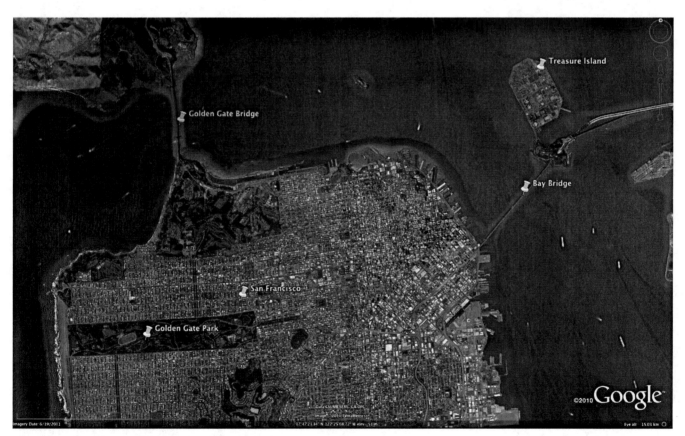

San Francisco, California

Name _____ Date _____

A Look from Above

 Describe the regions that you see in Google Earth using three adjectives: one to describe color, one to describe the shape or texture, and one to describe your feelings or impressions about the feature.

Feature	Color	Shape or Texture	Feeling or Impression
desert			
island			
forest			
ocean			
ice- or snow- covered area			

 Color Africa using the colors as they appear on the Google Earth globe. Then, label a desert, a forest, an island, and the oceans.

A Look from Above *(cont.)*

3 On the lines below, describe what each color suggests about Africa's features.

green _____

blue _____

brown _____

tan _____

white _____

4 Zoom in until you can no longer see the edges of the Earth. Click and hold the small arrow at the top of the Look joystick until Earth's horizon is in view. Describe how this view of Earth is different from the view of the whole Earth.

_____

_____

_____

5 Label the description of each tool with the corresponding letter on the diagram.

a

c

b

_____ This tool lets you look around as if you were turning your head.

_____ This tool moves your position over the Earth.

_____ This tool rotates your view relative to North.

Searching to Find Me

Standard
Students know major physical and man-made features of places as they are represented on maps and globes.

Google Earth Tools

- Search panel: Fly to box*

Overview

Students will continue to learn to use the basic Google Earth tools by searching for and exploring the Statue of Liberty and their school. Students will learn to distinguish their school from other structures in a city.

Vocabulary

- characteristic
- geometric

Materials

- *My Community* activity sheets (pages 41–42)
- a book, a box, or other three-dimensional object

Procedure

1 Set a book, a box, or another three-dimensional object on a table and ask students to consider how it would appear from a bird's-eye view. Ask students how they think their school might look to a bird in flight. How might a bird recognize a school from all the other buildings in a town?

2 Distribute copies of the *My Community* activity sheets (pages 41–42) to students and open Google Earth.

3 Show students that the upper-left portion of the **Google Earth Window** contains the **Search panel**. (***Note:*** Make sure the **Fly To tab** is selected, not the **Find Businesses** or the **Find Directions tabs**.)

4 Point out the **Fly to box.** Type "Statue of Liberty, New York City, New York" in the **Fly to box** and click the magnifying glass to begin your search. (***Note:*** Emphasize the need to include the name of the place, city, and state or country in the **Fly to box.**)

* Tool introduced in this lesson

Searching to Find Me *(cont.)*

Procedure *(cont.)*

5 Point out some of the features of the Statue of Liberty as it appears in the **3D viewer**. Ask students to count the geometric shapes they see around the Statue of Liberty and to record the numbers on their activity sheets (question 1).

6 Type the name of your city and state (e.g., Pasadena, California) or city and country (e.g., Rome, Italy) in the **Fly to box** and click the magnifying glass to search. **Zoom** in to a view that allows you to point out some familiar features, such as landmarks or buildings, to orient students. Ask students to write down at least three features or places that they recognize (question 2).

7 Type the address of your school in the **Fly to box** and hit the Enter or Return key. (**Note:** This is an alternative search method to clicking the magnifying glass.) Have students use the **zoom** and cursor to hunt for the objects listed on their activity sheets (question 3) (e.g., the playground, the field, the buildings, the road, the lunch area, and the parking lot). Have students choose an object to sketch as seen from ground-level and above ground-level (question 4).

8 Tell students that their school is one of thousands in the world. On the activity sheet (question 5) are some other schools from the United States. Ask students to **Fly to** these schools and list features of these schools that are similar to and different from their school (question 5).

9 After searching for schools around the United States, ask students to write three common characteristics of schools as seen in Google Earth that would help them recognize any school around the world (question 6).

Searching to Find Me *(cont.)*

Extension Activities

- Your city is probably not the oldest, the highest, the largest, or the smallest city in the world. Here are some record-holding cities. Have students **Fly to** these cities and use the **navigation tools** to find unique characteristics. Ask students to keep a record of these features on a chart on the board.

  ➤ Beijing, China (most populated city)

  ➤ Buford, Wyoming (least populated city in the United States with a population of 1)

  ➤ Byblos, Lebanon (oldest city; **Fly to** Byblos Crusader Castle to find the original city)

  ➤ Jiang Nan Wen Ti Zhuan Mai, Tibet, China (highest city at 4280 m or 14,044 ft. elevation)

- Use the **Fly to box** to find the Empire State Building, New York City, New York. **Zoom** in and use the **Look joystick** to explore the area around the Empire State Building. Ask students why all the buildings look flat against the ground.

Did You Know? ⊗

Astronauts take hundreds of photographs of Earth while on their missions. Some of their favorite places to photograph are Manicouagan, Canada; Crater Lake, Oregon; and Hawaii. Why do you think astronauts are interested in these locations?

User Tip

Sometimes typing only the name of a famous place in the **Fly to box** is enough to find that place. Other times, you need to add the city and state or country. In most cases, you will need to use your **navigation tools** to provide a recognizable and interesting view.

Searching to Find Me *(cont.)*

Screenshots

Search panel, Fly To Tab, and Fly to box

Liberty Island, New York City, New York

Name _____ Date _____

My Community

 1 Look at the Statue of Liberty in Google Earth. How many of each shape do you see?

_____ circles

_____ squares

_____ rectangles

_____ triangles

List other shapes you see: _____

 2 Look at your city in Google Earth. Write at least three features in your city that you recognize.

_____

_____

_____

 3 In Google Earth, use the zoom and cursor to look around your school for the objects listed below. Place a check mark next to the objects you find.

_____ playground   _____ road

_____ field   _____ lunch area

_____ buildings   _____ parking lot

My Community *(cont.)*

4 Sketch one of the objects you found at your school. Draw it as seen from above and from the ground. Show your sketches to a classmate and see if they can guess what you drew.

From Above   From the Ground

The object is: _____

5 Fly to the following schools:

- George Washington Elementary School, Baltimore, Maryland
- George Washington Elementary School, Mohegan Lake, New York
- George Washington Elementary School, Burbank, California

How are these schools similar to yours? How are they different?

_____

_____

_____

6 Write three common characteristics of schools as seen in Google Earth that would help you recognize any school around the world.

_____

_____

_____

Saving Your Place

Google Earth Tools

- Toolbar: Placemark*

Overview

Students will use basic Google Earth tools to explore the pyramids of Egypt and their surrounding features. They will learn what a river's floodplain and delta look like compared to a desert, and learn that people can live in both environments.

Vocabulary

- agriculture
- delta
- floodplain
- pharaoh

Materials

- *Placemarking the Pyramids* activity sheets (pages 47–48)
- crayons or colored pencils
- a bowl of salt
- glue sticks
- pictures or books about Egypt (optional)

Procedure

1. Talk about some of the places students discovered in the previous lessons. Encourage students to use interesting adjectives to describe these places. Show students some pictures of ancient Egypt (see the Recommended Literature list on page 243 or on the Teacher Resource CD). Ask students what they think the Nile River, the pyramids, and the Sahara Desert might look like in Google Earth.

2. Distribute copies of the *Placemarking the Pyramids* activity sheets (pages 47–48) to students and open Google Earth.

3. Turn off all the layers in the **Layers panel** (you can do this by turning off **Primary Database**). **Fly to** the Great Pyramid of Giza, Egypt. A list of nearby locations with **red balloon icons** will appear in a box directly below the **Search panel**. In the box, double-click on "Great Pyramid of Giza" to **zoom** to that location. Close the pop-up window that opens in the **3D viewer** by clicking the X. **Zoom** out until two large pyramids and one smaller pyramid fill the screen. On their activity sheets, have students label and color the pyramids, the desert, and the populated areas of the map. Then, have students answer question 1.

* Tool introduced in this lesson

Saving Your Place *(cont.)*

Procedure *(cont.)*

4 Students may want to keep the interesting places they find in Google Earth for future reference. Tell students they can **placemark** a site. Using the cursor, click on the **placemark tool** in the **Toolbar** (the yellow thumbtack) at the top of the **3D viewer**. A yellow thumbtack, or **placemark icon**, with a flashing square around it will appear in the **3D viewer**, along with a **Placemark window**.

5 Drag the **placemark icon** to a location on or near Khufu's Pyramid—the northernmost large pyramid. Type "Great Pyramid of Giza, Egypt" in the **Name box** in the **Placemark window** and click **OK**. Look in the **Search panel** for your **placemark**—it will have a yellow thumbtack next to it. Drag the **placemark** to the **My Places folder** in the **Places panel** to save it (see User Tips). If you need to move the **placemark**, right-click on it and select **Get Info** (Mac) or **Properties** (PC) to open the **Placemark window**. (*Note:* placemarks can only be moved when their **Placemark window** is open.) Ask students to draw a yellow thumbtack on Khufu's pyramid on the map on their activity sheets (question 2).

6 **Zoom** in so only Khufu's pyramid and its surrounding structures fill the **3D viewer**. The three smaller pyramids just to the east of Khufu's pyramid are the Queens' Pyramids; they are much more eroded than the pharaohs' pyramids. Ask a student to point to these and then **placemark** them by putting the **placemark icon** on the center pyramid. Ask students to answer question 3 on their activity sheets about who they think Egyptians considered more important—men or women?

7 Ask students to come up and use the **Move joystick** to move east into the city, and to **zoom** in until they have a clear view of the neighborhood. Ask students to compare this city to their city. On their activity sheets, have students describe this neighborhood and write what they think the dominant colors represent (question 4).

8 **Zoom** out until the Nile River is visible (it is east of the pyramids). Point out the green floodplain where the river floods annually to provide water to the vegetation, and the desert. Discuss why the floodplain is important to Egypt's agriculture. **Placemark** the Nile River. This time, choose a different **placemark icon**. Click on the yellow thumbtack to the right of the **Name box** to open the **icon window** with a wide selection of icon options.

Saving Your Place *(cont.)*

Procedure *(cont.)*

Click on one to select it, then click **OK** in the **icon window**, and then **OK** in the **Placemark window**. Drag the **placemark** to the **My Places folder** in the **Places panel**. Ask students to draw a simple icon that might represent their school on their activity sheets (question 5).

 Zoom out until students see the green delta (the Nile Delta) to the north, the sand-colored Sahara Desert to the west, and part of the blue Mediterranean Sea to the north. **Placemark** these locations and add them to the **My Places folder**. Discuss how a delta is formed. Ask students to label and color the maps on their activity sheets (question 6). Ask students to draw an arrow on the map to show which way the water flows along the Nile.

Extension Activities

- Have students paste some salt on the salty water in their pictures (the Mediterranean Sea) using their glue sticks, but to avoid putting salt on the Nile River, as this is fresh water.

- **Placemark** your school and drag it to the **My Places folder**. Compare the neighborhood around your school to the neighborhood east of the pyramids. Look for features they may have in common, such as golf courses, swimming pools, parks, or roads, and choose icons to represent each feature.

User Tips

To save **placemarks**, drag them from the **Search panel** to the **Places panel** and drop them in the **My Places folder**. The **placemarks** will now appear every time this computer is turned on; **placemarks** left in the **Search panel** will be deleted when Google Earth is closed.

Sometimes when you type a name in the **Placemark window**, the name will change to "Untitled Placemark" when you close the window. To avoid this, click once in the **Description box** or add a description before closing the **Placemark window**.

Saving Your Place *(cont.)*

Screenshots

Placemark tool

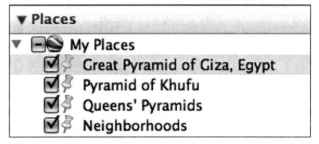

Places panel

Great Pyramid of Giza, Egypt

Name _____ Date _____

Placemarking the Pyramids

 Label and color the map below to show the desert, the pyramids, and populated areas. Then answer the questions below.

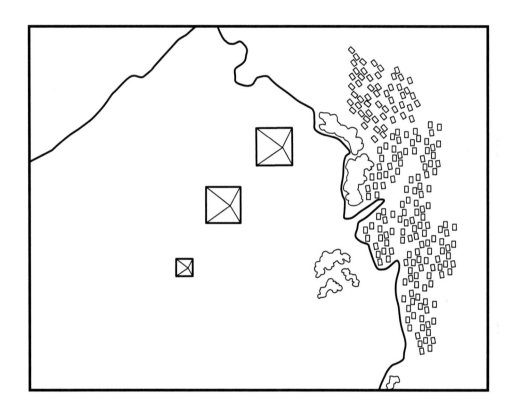

What is the shape of the pyramid base?

_____

How many sides do the pyramids have?

_____

 On the map above, draw the thumbtack that represents a placemark for Khufu's pyramid in Google Earth.

Placemarking the Pyramids *(cont.)*

3 Look at the pharaohs' pyramids and the queens' pyramids. Who do you think were more important to the Egyptians, men or women? How do you know?

_____

_____

4 Describe the neighborhood east of the pyramids. What do the dominant colors represent?

_____

_____

_____

_____

5 Draw a placemark icon that might represent your school.

6 Label the following on the map at right:

- Nile River
- Nile Delta
- Sahara Desert
- Mediterranean Sea

Color the water. Draw an arrow to show which way the water flows in the Nile.

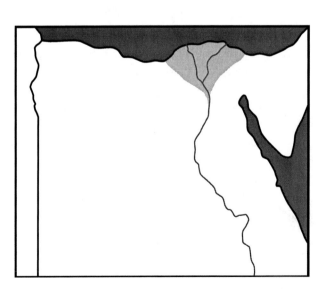

Exploring with Layers

Standard
Students know that physical
systems affect human systems.

Google Earth Tools

- Layers panel: Borders and Labels*
- Layers panel: Photos*
- Layers panel: 3D Buildings*
- Layers panel: More: Wikipedia*
- Places panel: My Places folder*
- Toolbar: Placemark

Overview

Students will use the creative data sets provided in the Layers panel to learn about important landmarks and the geographic features that contributed to their locations.

Vocabulary

- cathedral
- landmark

Materials

- *World in 3D* activity sheet (pages 53–54)
- highlighters

Procedure

1 Show students a picture of the Notre Dame Cathedral in Paris. Ask students how they might learn more about it (*encyclopedias, library, Internet, books*).

2 Distribute copies of the *World in 3D* activity sheets (pages 53–54) to students and open Google Earth.

3 **Fly to** Cathedrale Notre-Dame de Paris, France. (***Note:*** You may see many choices in the box below the **Search panel**. Double-click on "Cathedrale Notre-Dame de Paris.") Close the pop-up window and **balloon icons** by turning off the boxes in the **Search panel**, and use the **navigation tools** to center Notre Dame in the **3D viewer**. Point out the cathedral and ask students if it is in the city or the countryside of Paris. Ask them to describe its special location in Paris. **Zoom** in and out to see Paris and its surrounding region. Tell students that the island on which Notre Dame sits originally made transportation across the Seine River easier and was one reason why the city of Paris developed where it did.

* Tool introduced in this lesson

Exploring with Layers *(cont.)*

Procedure *(cont.)*

4 **Placemark** Notre Dame and move it to the **My Places folder**. **Zoom** in so the cathedral fills the **3D viewer**. Tell students this is a famous landmark. Have them write their own definition for landmark on their activity sheets (question 1).

5 **Zoom** out until the entire island on which Notre Dame sits, Isle de Cite, fills the **3D viewer**. Look in the **Layers panel** under **Primary Database** for the **Photos layer**. Click the small box to the left of **Photos** to turn this layer on. Ask students to look in the **3D viewer** for the small **photo icons**. Click on some of them to get an idea of what they represent. Tell students that these are photos people have taken of Notre Dame and added to Google Earth.

6 Click on one of the **photo icons** to open a pop-up window and view the photo. Then, click on the photo in the pop-up window to view the photo in an **Internet viewer**. Have students click on three different **photo icons** near Notre Dame Cathedral and draw what they see in the **Internet viewer** (question 2).

7 Turn off the **Photos layer** and look in the **Layers panel** for the **3D Buildings layer**. Turn on this layer and use the **navigation tools** to explore Notre Dame in 3D. **Zoom** in close and use the top arrow on the **Look joystick** to "look up" at the building. Use the left and right arrows to look around. Use the **Move joystick** to travel.

8 Turn off the **3D Buildings layer** and navigate back to a view from above. Look in the **More layer** for the **Wikipedia layer**. Turn on this layer and then locate and click on the **Wikipedia icon** for Notre Dame. Ask all students to read the information in the window and write down something they have learned about Notre Dame from Wikipedia on their activity sheets (question 3).

9 Turn off the **Wikipedia layer** and **zoom** out so most of Europe is in the **3D viewer**. Turn on the **Borders and Labels layer** in the **Layers panel** and **zoom** in until the names of countries are visible.

Exploring with Layers *(cont.)*

Procedure *(cont.)*

10 Ask students what they think the red stars represent in each country and to write their guesses on their activity sheets (question 4). Tell students that the red stars are capital cities. Ask students to look for the capitals of Belgium and Switzerland and write them on their activity sheets (question 5).

11 With students, navigate over Europe and find three interesting landmarks by turning on the **Places layer**. Use the **3D Buildings**, **Photos**, and **Wikipedia layers** to learn about each landmark. Have students write the name of each landmark on their activity sheets, along with one piece of information they learned (question 6).

Extension Activity

Explore the area near the Gateway Arch in St. Louis, Missouri. Have students use the **Places layer** to identify features such as baseball stadiums, parks, and museums. Use the **Wikipedia layer** to find out what the arch symbolizes and why it is an important landmark.

User Tip

The **3D Buildings layer** should be deselected when not in use because it slows down Google Earth.

Did You Know? ⊗

Wikipedia is an open-source encyclopedia that is always being updated and anyone can contribute information, so it is not considered an authoritative source. Google Earth has open-source features, too. Three-dimensional models of buildings are made by many different users and added to Google Earth.

Exploring with Layers *(cont.)*

Screenshots

Isle De Cite, Paris, France

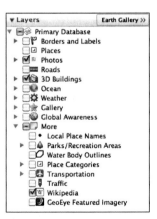

Layers Panel

Name _____ Date _____

World in 3D

1 Write your own definition of a *landmark*.

_____

2 Click on three different photo icons near the Notre Dame Cathedral. Draw what you see in the boxes below, and then write what appears in each photo on the lines below.

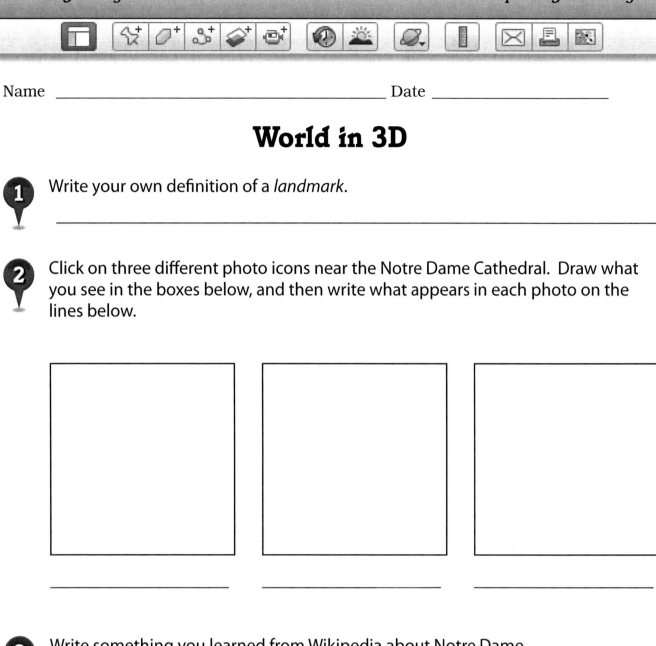

_____ _____ _____

3 Write something you learned from Wikipedia about Notre Dame.

_____

_____

_____

World in 3D *(cont.)*

4 Zoom out to see more European countries. What do you think the red stars represent in Google Earth?

_____

5 What is the capital of Belgium? _____

What is the capital of Switzerland? _____

6 Find three interesting landmarks in Europe. Write something you learned about these landmarks using Google Earth layers.

Landmark: _____

Information: _____

_____

Landmark: _____

Information: _____

_____

Landmark: _____

Information: _____

_____

Identifying Artificial Features

Standard
Students understand how physical processes help to shape features and patterns on Earth's surface.

Google Earth Tools

- Layers panel: Places*
- Toolbar: Placemark
- Places panel: My Places folder
- Status bar: Eye alt*

Overview

Students will investigate artificial, or man-made, features.

Vocabulary

- altitude
- structure

Materials

- *Walls All Around* activity sheets (pages 58–60)

Procedure

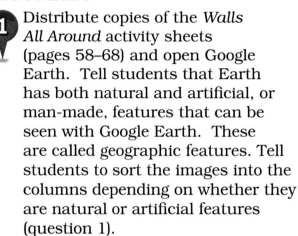

1 Distribute copies of the *Walls All Around* activity sheets (pages 58–68) and open Google Earth. Tell students that Earth has both natural and artificial, or man-made, features that can be seen with Google Earth. These are called geographic features. Tell students to sort the images into the columns depending on whether they are natural or artificial features (question 1).

2 Turn off all **Layers** in the **Layers panel** and all **Places** in the **Places panel**. **Zoom** out to the smallest view of Earth. Show students the **Eye alt** in the **Status bar** at the bottom of the **3D viewer**. Tell students that **Eye alt** indicates the height, or altitude, of your eye above the surface of Earth. More specifically, it is the height above sea level. It should currently be about 64,000 km (40,000 mi.), which is only about $\frac{1}{6}$ of the distance to the Moon. Ask students what features they see that are man-made. Continue zooming in to lower altitudes. On their activity sheets, have students write at what height they were able to start seeing man-made features (question 2).

* Tool introduced in this lesson

Identifying Artificial Features *(cont.)*

Procedure *(cont.)*

3 One feature that many people believe is visible from space is the Great Wall of China. Show students the actual **Eye alt** at which the Great Wall is visible by flying to Jiayuguan, China, and turning on the **Places layer** in the **Layers panel**. **Zoom** in on the **place icon** representing the "Jiayuguan Cultural Relics Scenic Area" and look just to the west for the Jiayu Pass, a square structure just outside the green area. The Great Wall extends north and south of this first pass. Center the pass in the **3D viewer** and **zoom** to an **Eye alt** of about 2 km (7,500 ft.). **Placemark** the pass and add it to your **My Places folder**.

4 **Zoom** out until it is no longer possible to see the wall. Ask students to write on their activity sheets the **Eye alt** at which the wall disappears (question 3). Their activity sheet lists the altitude of the Space Shuttle 320 km (200 mi.) and Apollo on the Moon 400,000 km (250,000 mi.). Ask students if they think the Great Wall could have been seen from the moon or the Space Shuttle.

5 Tell students that a wall was a common structure of many early settlements for the protection it offered. **Fly to** and **placemark** the locations listed on students' activity sheets, and have students describe the kind of protection each wall offered (question 4). Move the placemarks into the **My Places folder** in the **Places panel**.

6 **Zoom** in to get a closer look at each wall. Have students fill out the triple Venn diagram on their activity sheets (question 5) to compare the three walls. Students should write the common features in the overlapping sections of the diagram, and features unique to each wall in the outside circles.

7 Have students work with partners to write a paragraph on their activity sheets comparing the walls (question 6). Ask them why they think the wall around Plimoth Plantation was less sophisticated than the walls around Xian and Beaumaris Castle, even though it was built hundreds of years later.

Identifying Artificial Features *(cont.)*

Extension Activities

- The boundaries of cities are also protected by natural features, such as mountains, rivers, and oceans. Ask students to **Fly to** Potala, Lhasa, China and **placemark** it at an **Eye alt** of 6 km (20,000 ft.). This was once the chief residence of the Dalai Lama. **Zoom** out to see the city of Lhasa and the surrounding mountains. Ask students to point out the boundaries that currently limit this city's expansion (mountains).

- Ask students to return to the Great Wall of China and **zoom** out to an **Eye alt** of about 27 km (17 mi.). Have students find other linear (straight and curved) features in the desert. Ask students to identify these and determine if they are natural or artificial features. Students should be able to find a river, a highway, a road, and a railroad track.

Screenshot

Jiayu Pass, China

Name _____ Date _____

Walls All Around

 1 Look at the pictures below. Decide if each feature is natural or articifial. Then, write the name of each feature in the correct column below.

Natural Features	Artificial Features

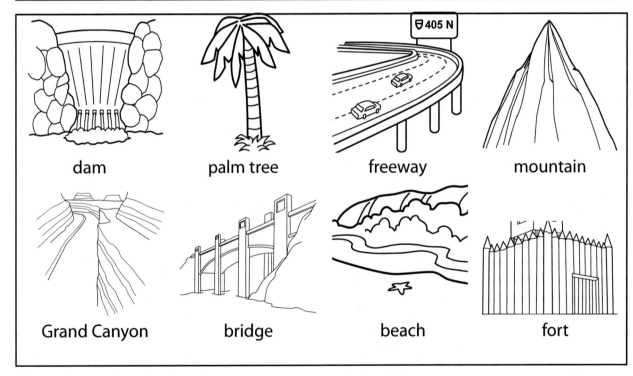

dam   palm tree   freeway   mountain

Grand Canyon   bridge   beach   fort

 2 Start at the farthest altitude away from Earth and slowly zoom in to lower altitudes. Write the Eye alt at which you are able to start seeing artificial features.

_____ Eye alt

Walls All Around *(cont.)*

3 Zoom out slowly from the Great Wall of China until it is no longer possible to see the wall. Write the Eye alt at which the wall disappears. _____ Eye alt

Earth as seen from the Space Shuttle at 320 km (200 mi.)

Earth as seen from Apollo at 400,000 km (250,000 mi.)

Do you think astronauts on the Moon or orbiting in the Space Shuttle could see the Great Wall of China? Why or why not? Use the information above to help you answer this question.

_____

_____

4 Look at and placemark the following locations at the suggested Eye alt. On the lines below each location, describe the kind of protection that each wall offered.

• Xian, China (Eye alt: 6 km or 20,000 ft.): One of the oldest Chinese city walls; built about 1370 A.D.

_____

• Beaumaris Castle, Beaumaris, United Kingdom (Eye alt: 365 m or 1,200 ft.): A typical medieval castle; built about 1295 A.D.

_____

• Plimoth Plantation, Plymouth, MA (Eye alt: 24 m or 800 ft.): A re-creation of the real Plimoth; originally built in 1620 A.D.

_____

Walls All Around *(cont.)*

5 Fill out the triple Venn diagram below to compare the three walls. Write the common features in the overlapping sections of the diagram, and features unique to each wall in the outside circles.

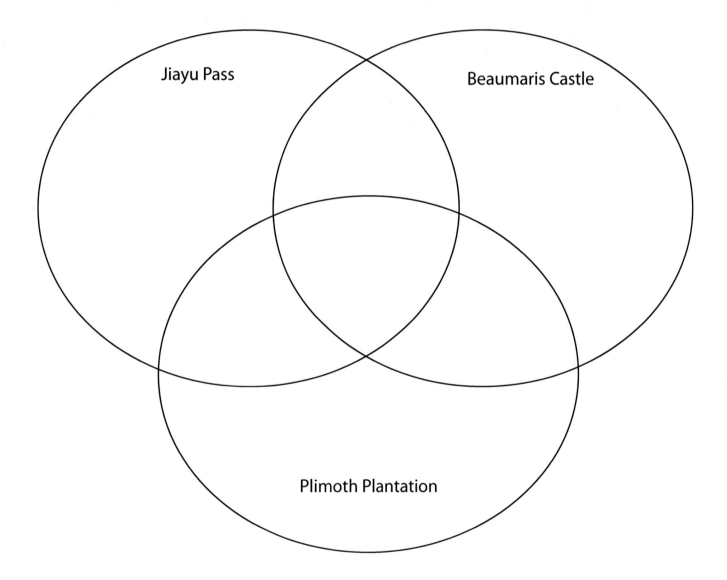

6 Work with a partner to write a paragraph (on a separate piece of paper) comparing the walls. Why do you think the wall around Plimoth Plantation is not as strong or modern-looking as the walls around Xian and Beaumaris Castle, even though it was built hundreds of years later?

Investigating Natural Features

Standard
Students know the physical processes that shape patterns on Earth's surface.

Google Earth Tools
- Status bar: elev*
- Status bar: Eye alt
- Toolbar: Clock*
- Toolbar: Placemark

Overview
Students will investigate natural features, including landforms and ecosystems.

Vocabulary
- elevation
- erosion
- magma
- volcano

Materials
- *Elevation Situation* activity sheets (pages 64–66)
- colored pencils or crayons

* Tool introduced in this lesson

Procedure

1 Tell students that natural features include landforms, such as terrain and water bodies, and ecosystems, such as forests and grasslands. Distribute copies of the *Elevation Situation* activity sheets (pages 64–66) to students, and have them label the natural feature in each photograph (question 1).

2 Open Google Earth. **Fly to** Egmont National Park, New Zealand. The main feature of this park is Mt. Taranaki, a perfectly formed volcano. **Zoom** to a view in which the volcano fills the **3D viewer** (an **Eye alt** of about 9 km or 30,000 ft.). On their activity sheets, have students list the natural features they see on and around Mt. Taranaki, such as forests, rivers, or canyons (question 2). (***Note:*** Depending on the time of year the images were taken, students may see snow covering the volcano.)

3 Tell students that Mt. Taranaki is a volcano, which is a landform that is created when magma (liquid rock) rises to the surface of our planet. Over time, the magma cools into rock, and then snow builds up at the summit, sometimes forming a glacier, or a large body of ice moving down a valley. The ice and snow will eventually melt, eroding the volcano. Ask students to look for signs of erosion on Mt. Taranaki. Have students describe these signs and answer question 3 on their activity sheets.

Investigating Natural Features (cont.)

Procedure (cont.)

4 Keep the volcano in the center of the **3D viewer** and **zoom** out to an **Eye alt** of about 30 km (20 mi.). Large rectangular regions and a large circular region should be visible. Tell students the large rectangular region is the boundary of an image that was taken at a different time or with a different instrument than the images that make up the rest of the region. The large circular region is the boundary of the park. **Zoom** in to investigate the park boundary and ask students to determine the difference between the natural features inside and outside the park.

5 Point out the **elev** on the **Status bar**. Tell students it stands for elevation, which is the height of the land above sea level. Have students write the definition for elevation on their activity sheets (question 4). Remind students that **Eye alt** is the height of your eye above sea level as you **zoom** in and out, and **elev** is the actual height of the surface you are viewing above sea level.

6 Without clicking it or dragging it, move the cursor across the span of Mt. Taranaki, and notice how the **elev** changes but the **Eye alt** does not. Ask students what they think the highest and lowest points on the volcano are, and to place their cursors on those points (highest then lowest).

7 Measure the **elev** for the points around the park that are marked on the diagram on students' activity sheets. Ask students to write these elevations on their diagrams and describe the natural features at each elevation (question 5).

8 Have students work with partners to find the natural features listed on their activity sheets (question 6). Tell partners to **Fly to** each feature and **zoom** to the specified **Eye alt**. Ask each pair to **placemark** the features and use **elev** to find the highest and lowest elevations around each feature.

9 Ask several pairs of students to come up and point out a feature they investigated from question 6. Ask students to discuss how they think the feature was formed. Encourage students to include in their discussions the importance of elevation change to erosion.

Investigating Natural Features *(cont.)*

Extension Activity

Have students find and placemark natural features such as volcanoes, islands, capes, peninsulas, canyons, plateaus, and dunes and bodies of water such as gulfs, bays, deltas, rivers, lakes, and glaciers. What are the characteristics of the different ecosystems as seen in Google Earth?

User Tip

In version 6.0 of Google Earth, the **Terrain** feature is on by default; in earlier versions of Google Earth, students will need to go to the **Layers panel**, open the **More layer**, and turn on the **Terrain layer**.

Did You Know? ⊗

A landform can get its shape from both constructive forces, like magma rising to form a volcano, and destructive forces, like erosion from melting glaciers.

Screenshot

Egmont National Park

Mt. Taranaki

Park boundary

©2011 GeoEye, ©2011 WhereIs® Sensis Pty Ltd, Image Taranaki Regional/Stratford/South Taranaki Councils

Mt. Taranaki, Egmont Park, New Zealand

Name _____ Date _____

Elevation Situation

1 Label each picture below with one of these types of natural features: *forest, volcano, plateau, river.*

_____

_____

_____

_____

2 Zoom in and look around Mt. Taranaki at Egmont National Park in New Zealand. List the natural features you see on and around this volcano.

_____

_____

3 What are the signs of erosion on Mt. Taranaki? What natural feature forms when snow on mountains melts?

_____

_____

Elevation Situation (cont.)

4 Define *elevation*: _____

5 Fill in the elevations marked on the picture below and describe the natural features at each elevation.

Elevation Situation *(cont.)*

 6 Fly to the following locations. Then, fill in the blanks in the chart below to identify the natural feature, and the highest and lowest elevation at each location.

Natural Feature	Location	Eye alt	Highest Elevation	Lowest Elevation
	Matterhorn, Italy	6 km (20,000 ft.)		
	North Aral Sea, Kazakhstan	150 km (95 mi.)		
	Fernandina, Ecuador	40 km (25 mi.)		
	Grand Canyon, Arizona	40 km (20 mi.)		

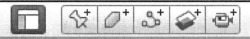

Overlaying Abstract Features

Standard

Students use map grids (e.g., latitude and longitude or alphanumeric system) to plot absolute location.

Google Earth Tools

- Layers panel: Borders and Labels, Places
- Status bar: Eye alt
- Status bar: lat/long*
- View: Grid*

Overview

Students will use Google Earth to investigate the abstract features of latitude and longitude.

Vocabulary

- horizontal
- intersecting
- latitude
- longitude
- parallel
- vertical

Materials

- *Lines Around Earth* activity sheets (pages 71–72)
- highlighters

Procedure

1. Tell students that abstract features, like borders, the Equator, and lines of latitude and longitude, are used on maps, but are not visible on Earth.

2. Distribute copies of the *Lines Around Earth* activity sheets (pages 71–72) and open Google Earth. Navigate to Africa at an **Eye alt** of about 9,000 km (6,000 mi.). Click on **View** in the **Menu Bar**, and then choose **Grid** to turn on the latitude/longitude grid. Explain to students that in a North-up view, latitude lines are horizontal and longitude lines are vertical. Tell students to label the latitude and longitude lines on the globe on their activity sheets (question 1).

3. Point out the Equator to students and show them how it encircles Earth like a belt and divides Earth into two halves. You can rotate the Earth in the **3D viewer** along the Equator by dragging a point along the Equator with your cursor.

* Tool introduced in this lesson

Overlaying Abstract Features *(cont.)*

Procedure *(cont.)*

4 Fly to Galapagos Islands, Ecuador and **zoom** in over the Equator line. Turn the **Grid** on and off. Ask students if they can see evidence of the Equator on the land or ocean. Have students highlight the Equator on their activity sheets (question 2).

5 Click the N in the **North-up button** to return the Earth to a North-up position. **Zoom** out to view the whole Earth and point out the Tropic of Cancer (above the Equator) and the Tropic of Capricorn (below the Equator). Tell students that between these lines, the sun shines directly overhead at least some of the year. North of the Tropic of Cancer and south of the Tropic of Capricorn, the sun always shines at an angle. Have students highlight and label the Tropic lines on the Earth on their activity sheets (question 3).

6 Use the **navigation tools** to rotate Earth to a view of the North Pole so the Earth fills the **3D viewer**. Discuss the differences between latitude and longitude lines at the pole. Have students label the latitude and longitude lines on the globe on their activity sheets (question 4). Have students write which lines are parallel and which are intersecting at the pole (question 5).

7 Point out the Arctic Circle. Tell students that within this circle, there are days when the sun never appears above the horizon—or the boundary between land and sky— and days when the sun never sets.

8 Navigate to the South Pole at an **Eye alt** of about 8,000 km (5,000 mi.). Ask students to use what they learned about the Arctic Circle to complete the sentence about the Antarctic Circle (question 6).

9 Tell students that specific latitude and longitude (**lat/long**) points are useful for finding locations when there are no specific names that you can enter in the **Fly to box**. Show students the **lat/long** display in the **Status bar** and explain that this shows the exact latitude and longitude of the cursor.

10 Show students how to turn on **Borders and Labels** and **Places** in the **Layers panel** by checking the box. Have students practice using latitude and longitude to view the locations on their activity sheets and answer question 7. See the *User Tips* on the next page for more information.

Overlaying Abstract Features *(cont.)*

Extension Activity

Look at the list of natural features below. **Fly to** each latitude, longitude, and **Eye alt** and add a **placemark** to your **My Places folder** using a **placemark icon** that best represents the feature. Use the **zoom** and **navigation tools** to look for evidence of human activity around each landform or ecosystem.

volcano	6 06 04 S	105 25 25 E	Eye alt 3 km (10,000 ft.)
river	39 42 27 N	91 20 29 W	Eye alt 5 km (16,500 ft.)
forest	48 00 42 N	8 15 51 E	Eye alt 2 km (6,500 ft.)

Did You Know?

Earth is not a perfect sphere, but bulges slightly at the Equator due to its rotation. The diameter of Earth at the Equator is approximately 43 km larger than the diameter through the poles. Because of this bulge, the farthest point from the center of Earth is the Chimborazo volcano in Ecuador.

User Tips

Entering latitude and longitude locations into the **Fly to box** can be tricky. It is not necessary to type in the symbols for degrees, minutes, and seconds—just type a space between each set of digits and letters. The easiest way to enter them correctly is to have one person read the location aloud while another person types (e.g. "Thirty-one, space, seventeen, space, forty-seven, space, letter S, space, one hundred seventy-four, space, three, space, fifty-three, space, letter E."

The latitude and longitude of the location (or **lat/long** in the **Status bar**) of the cursor is always displayed in the **status bar** at the bottom center of the **3D viewer**. When searching for a specific **lat/long**, it may not always appear in the center of the **3D viewer**. It may take some navigating to find the exact **lat/long** you are looking for.

Overlaying Abstract Features *(cont.)*

Screenshots

View	Tools	Add	Window	H
✓ Toolbar			⌥⌘T	
✓ Sidebar			⌥⌘B	
View Size			▶	
Show Navigation			▶	
✓ Status Bar				
Grid			⌘L	
Overview Map			⌥⇧⌘M	

View menu

32°15'51.50" N   99°44'55.92" E

lat/long display in Status bar

Grid view on

DATA SIO, NOAA, U.S. NAVY, NGA, GEBCO, ©2011 CNES/SPOT IMAGE, IMAGE IBCAO

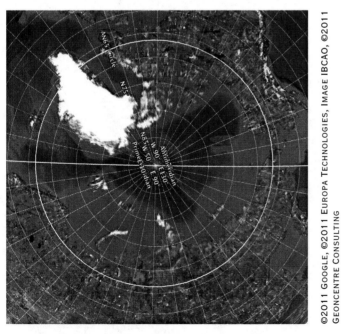

lat/long in polar view

©2011 GOOGLE, ©2011 EUROPA TECHNOLOGIES, IMAGE IBCAO, ©2011 GEONCENTRE CONSULTING

Name _____ Date _____

Lines Around Earth

1 Label lines of latitude and longitude on the globe below.

2 On the globe above, highlight and label the Equator.

3 On the globe above, highlight and label the Tropic of Cancer and the Tropic of Capricorn.

Lines Around Earth *(cont.)*

 Label lines of latitude and longitude on the polar view of the globe below.

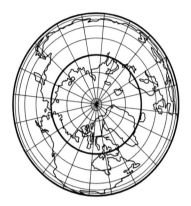

 At the pole, which lines are parallel and which are intersecting?

_____

_____

 Using what you learned about the Arctic Circle, complete the following sentence about the Antarctic Circle:

South of the Antarctic Circle, there are days when the sun _____

_____

 Step 1: Turn off Borders and Labels. Type 25 S 135 E in the Fly to box and zoom out slowly until you can see the entire continent. Turn on Borders and Labels in the Layers panel. What continent are you on?

_____

Step 2: Turn off Borders and Labels. Type 33 52 S 151 12 E in the Fly to box. Turn on Borders and Labels. What city do you see?

_____

Step 3: Turn off Borders and Labels. Type 33 51 08 S 151 12 38 E in the Fly to box. Turn on Places in the Layers panel. What structure do you see?

_____

Creating Reference Scales

Standard

Students understand the spatial organization of places through such concepts as location, distance, direction, scale, movement, and region.

Google Earth Tools

- Toolbar: Placemark
- Toolbar: Ruler*
- View: Scale Legend*

Overview

Students will use Google Earth to develop a reference scale that will allow them to compare the sizes of places they see in Google Earth with the size of their school.

Vocabulary

- reference
- scale

Materials

- *Comparing Sizes and Distances* activity sheets (pages 77–78)
- one blank 3" x 5" card for each student
- *Zoom* (Banyai 1998) (optional)

Procedure

1. Remind students of places they have already visited using Google Earth (pyramids, a volcano, a cathedral). Ask students if they think these places are bigger than their school. You may also read a book, like *Zoom* (Banyai 1998), and open a discussion about the scale of features. Ask students how they would go about determining the scale of features in Google Earth.

2. Explain to students that in Google Earth, the **zoom slider** does more than just **zoom** in and **zoom** out; it changes the height of your eye above the surface, and therefore changes the scale of features. Sometimes a famous structure can seem huge, but in reality, it is not much bigger than your school. Other times a landscape feature may not seem very big, but in reality several cities would fit into it.

3. Distribute copies of the *Comparing Sizes and Distances* activity sheets (pages 77–78) to students and open Google Earth.

* Tool introduced in this lesson

Creating Reference Scales *(cont.)*

Procedure *(cont.)*

4 **Fly to** Spiral Jetty, Utah, and **zoom** to an **Eye alt** of 300 m (5,500 ft.). Tell students that this is a work of art built from rocks. Ask students how big they think the jetty is.

Use the **ruler tool** to measure the diameter of Spiral Jetty. Click on the **ruler tool** in the **Toolbar** to open the **Ruler window**. Make sure you are measuring with the appropriate unit of measure (meters). Click once on one side of Spiral Jetty, then click again on the other side. You will see a line spanning the diameter of the jetty. In the **Ruler window,** the length of the line will be displayed. Select *meters* or *feet*. Have students record the measurement on the chart on their activity sheets (question 1).

Fly to your school and use the **ruler tool** to measure the width or length of your school building. Have students record this measurement on their activity sheets (question 2).

7 A classic method of estimating scale on maps is using the map legend to determine the appropriate scale. Click on **View** in the **Menu bar**, and select **Scale Legend**. The scale legend will appear in the lower left corner of the **3D viewer**. **Zoom** in or out until the **Scale Legend** reads approximately 100 m (300 ft.). Hold an index card up to the screen and mark the size of your school

building on the card. Label the card, "Our School Building at 100 m Scale."

8 **Fly to** Spiral Jetty (double-click on it in the **Search panel**), **zoom** until the **Scale Legend** reads approximately 100 m (300 ft.), and compare the size of your school building to Spiral Jetty using the reference card. Have students draw Spiral Jetty and their school building in scale using what they learned with the reference card (question 3).

9 Have students **Fly to, placemark**, and measure the following landmarks using the **ruler tool**, then fill in the chart on their actvity sheets. Students should also use the reference card to compare their school building to each landmark (question 5).

- Colosseum, Rome, Italy
- Meteor Crater, Arizona
- Uluru, Australia
- The Sphinx, Egypt
- Saint Basil's Cathedral, Moscow, Russia
- Stonehenge, England

Creating Reference Scales *(cont.)*

Extension Activity

Fly to Cairo and **placemark** it.
Fly to Aswan Dam and **placemark**
it as well. Navigate to a view of
the Nile River that includes both
Cairo and Aswan Dam **placemarks**
(**Eye alt** 900 km). A bird could fly
in a straight line from Cairo to the
Aswan Dam. Use the **ruler tool**
to find out how far the bird's trip
would be in miles (approximately
430 miles). A fish, however, would
have to travel by river. Click the
Path tab in the **Ruler window**.
Click once on Cairo to mark your
starting point. Click again farther
up the river. Click a third dot
farther up the Nile and continue
tracing the Nile in segments
until you reach the Aswan Dam.
Compare the total distance the fish
traveled (approximately 520 miles)
to the distance the bird traveled
(approximately 430 miles). Whose
trip was longer?

Did You Know?

Euclid, a famous mathematician,
said, "the shortest distance between
two points is a straight line."

User Tip

If you have an interactive whiteboard,
use the pen tool to create a reference
scale and store it as an object in your
gallery. When you use Google Earth,
zoom out to the determined scale and
drag the **reference scale** onto the
whiteboard to use as a reference.

Creating Reference Scales *(cont.)*

Screenshots

Scale Legend

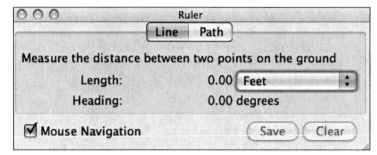

Ruler window

Spiral Jetty, Utah

Name _____ Date _____

Comparing Sizes and Distances

1 Use the ruler tool to measure the diameter of Spiral Jetty.

Diameter of Spiral Jetty: _____

2 Use the ruler tool to measure the width or length of your school campus.

Width or length of your school campus: _____

3 Draw your school and Spiral Jetty. Use the "Our School at 100 m Scale" reference card to help you draw them the correct size relative to each other.

Comparing Sizes and Distances *(cont.)*

 Fly to the locations listed in the chart below. Use the ruler tool to measure the length of diameter of each landmark and enter the measurements in the chart. Write whether each landmark is larger than, smaller than, or the same size as your school.

Landmark	Measurements	Is it larger or smaller than your school building, or the same size?
Colosseum, Rome, Italy		
Meteor Crater, Arizona		
Uluru, Australia		
The Sphinx, Egypt		
Saint Basil's Cathedral, Moscow, Russia		

Sorting Our Folders

Standard
Students understand the characteristics and uses of maps, globes, and other geographic tools and technologies.

Google Earth Tools
- Places panel: Folders*
- Toolbar: Placemark: Find*

Overview
Students will begin to develop a series of folders to save the places they visit in Google Earth.

Vocabulary
- category

Materials
- *Sorting Our World* activity sheets (pages 83–84)
- "Messy Room" (Silverstein 1981) (optional)

Procedure

1 Read the poem "Messy Room" (Silverstein 1981) or ask students to describe what their bedrooms look like when they get messy. Tell students that keeping track of all their **placemarks** in Google Earth can also get messy. It is helpful to build a system to organize their **placemarks**, not only to keep track of them, but to see relationships among the locations. Distribute copies of the *Sorting Our World* activity sheets (pages 83–84) to students and open Google Earth.

2 Show students how they can search for a **placemark** by clicking **Edit** in the **Menu Bar**, and selecting **Find**. In the **Find box**, type one or two letters of the **placemark** name and click the arrows to the search through the **placemarks** that have the same letters you typed into the **Find box**. The **placemark** will be highlighted (you may need to scroll to find it).

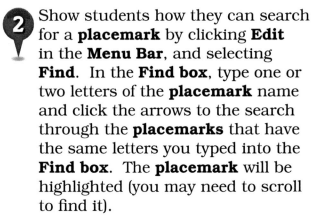

3 Tell students that they could also organize their **placemarks** in folders, just like they organize notebooks for school or files on a computer. Start with three folders called *Our Class*, *Our Library*, and *Our Studies*.

* Tool introduced in this lesson

Sorting Our Folders *(cont.)*

Procedure *(cont.)*

4 To create a new folder, right-click (or control-click) on the **My Places folder** at the top of the **Places panel** and select **Add**, and then select **Folder**. A **New Folder window** will appear that is similar to the **Placemark window**.

5 Type "Our Class" in the **Name box** and click **OK** to name and save the folder. This new folder will appear at the bottom of the list of **placemarks** in the **Places panel**. Move it to the top of the **panel** just under **My Places** by dragging it with the cursor. This folder will be one of three main category folders to collect all **placemarks** related directly to students, like the location of their school or places they have gone on field trips.

6 Highlight the **My Places folder** again and click **Add**, then select **Folder**. Add two more folders called *Our Library* and *Our Studies*. The *Our Library* folder will hold **placemarks** for places visited in literature, and the *Our Studies* folder will hold **placemarks** discovered while studying subjects in school like social studies and science.

7 On their activity sheets (question 1), ask students to create two subfolders under each main folder to provide a more organized sorting. For example, under the *Our Class* folder, students might add *Families* and *Fieldtrips*; under *Our Library*, they might add subfolders called *Fiction* and *Nonfiction*, or the names of favorite authors; and, under *Our Studies*, students might add folders called *Social Studies* and *Science*.

8 Add these subfolders in Google Earth by right-clicking on one of the three main level folders and choosing **Add**, then select **Folder**. Name each subfolder according to students' suggestions.

9 Drag each **placemark** for the locations you have investigated into the appropriate subfolder by clicking and holding it with the cursor, and then dragging it over the folder and releasing it. Continue to sort **placemarks** using student suggestions until all placemarks are in folders. Add additional folders as students suggest them.

Sorting Our Folders *(cont.)*

Procedure *(cont.)*

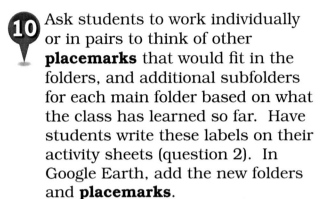 Ask students to work individually or in pairs to think of other **placemarks** that would fit in the folders, and additional subfolders for each main folder based on what the class has learned so far. Have students write these labels on their activity sheets (question 2). In Google Earth, add the new folders and **placemarks**.

Extension Activities

- Ask students to think of some places related to their own lives that they might like to add to a personal folder.
- Create more class folders to hold places your class discovers in social studies and science.

Did You Know?

When all the **placemarks** are on at once, students will see personal connections to the places they learn about in class and the places that they encounter in their own lives. They will also see cross-curricular connections. They may be surprised that people from their families live close to or at the locations from stories or from history. As students continue to "build their worlds," they will see the layers of connections grow!

User Tip

When you are selecting a place to drop a folder, a horizontal line appears as a placeholder in the **Places panel**. As you move the cursor left or right, the line gets longer or shorter depending on the folder level in which the paste will occur. Play with the line, dropping the folder when the line is different lengths, to get familiar with its length compared to where your **placemark** is inserted.

Sorting Our Folders *(cont.)*

Screenshots

Find in the Edit menu

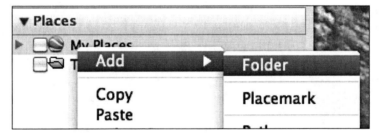

Add folder

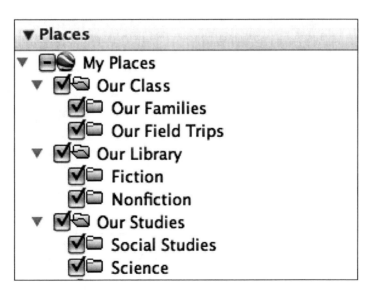

Class folders

Name _____ Date _____

Sorting Our World

1 In each main folder, think of two subfolders your class could use for sorting placemarks in Google Earth. Write the names for these subfolders below:

Main folder: *Our Class*

Subfolder:_____

Subfolder:_____

Main folder: *Our Library*

Subfolder:_____

Subfolder:_____

Main folder: *Our Studies*

Subfolder:_____

Subfolder:_____

Sorting Our World *(cont.)*

2 Write the names of some subfolders your class created. Then, write the names of some placemarks that go in each folder.

Main Folder: *Our Class*

    Subfolder: _____

        Placemarks: _____

        _____

    Subfolder: _____

        Placemarks: _____

        _____

Main Folder: *Our Library*

    Subfolder: _____

        Placemarks: _____

        _____

    Subfolder: _____

        Placemarks: _____

        _____

Main Folder: *Our Studies*

    Subfolder: _____

        Placemarks: _____

        _____

    Subfolder: _____

        Placemarks: _____

        _____

Following Our Family Trees

Standard
Students understand the nature and complexity of Earth's cultural mosaics.

Google Earth Tools

- Places panel: Folders
- Toolbar: Placemark

Overview

Students will develop personal Google Earth folders while exploring their own family trees.

Vocabulary

- maternal
- paternal

Materials

- *Back in Time* activity sheets (pages 88–90)
- markers

Procedure

Note: Before beginning this lesson, ask students to collect information from their parents or family members about their histories, including where they were born, cities they lived in, places they traveled, or where they attended school.

1. Talk about where students' relatives lived and grew up. Talk about family trees and how they are organized. Tell students that they will look for places where their relatives lived using Google Earth and will **placemark** and organize the places in folders to connect their own personal histories with the history they learn about in their textbooks and with each other.

2. Distribute copies of the *Back in Time* activity sheets (pages 88–90) to students and open Google Earth. Create a new folder titled *Our Families* under *Our Class* in the **Places panel**. Tell students they will learn how to create their own *My Family* folder by using an imaginary person and his or her imaginary family first.

Following Our Family Trees *(cont.)*

Procedure *(cont.)*

3 Select an imaginary character for your class family tree—perhaps a character from literature or a figure from history. You can have students research a historical character and provide factual information, or select a fictional character and create the information. Have students fill in the family tree for the character on their activity sheets, making sure to distinguish between the maternal and paternal relatives (question 1). In the chart, have students fill in the birthplace and birth year of each character (question 2).

4 **Placemark** each birthplace and give the **placemarks** unique titles that include the name of the person and the year they were born (e.g., George Washington, born 1732).

5 Create a subfolder under *Our Class* for this imaginary or historical family. Add a folder for each family member and move the **placemarks** into these.

6 For each family member, have students do an Internet search to look up major historical events that occurred during those years and during that person's lifetime. Have students record at least one event next to each family member on the chart on their activity sheets (question 2).

7 Have students create a personal family tree on their activity sheets (question 3) and fill in the chart (question 4).

8 If students have access to computers, ask them to **placemark** the locations from their own family histories in Google Earth, and have them organize their **placemarks** in their own *Me* folder under a new subfolder named *My Family*. If students are sharing computers, they should label the folders with their own names.

9 On a separate sheet of paper, have students write a one-page story about their families and the journeys that have led them here using something they learned from Google Earth (question 5).

Following Our Family Trees *(cont.)*

Extension Activities

- Have students share the places they have placemarked with relatives. They may have some ideas about other **placemarks** to add to the family folders. Ask students to write a paragraph explaining something they learned from their relatives about locations related to their family.

- Ask students to investigate the natural features in the area where one relative lives (or used to live). Then have students compare these natural features to those surrounding students' current homes, or compare how they looked in the past to how they look today. Have students write a paragraph describing the differences.

Screenshot

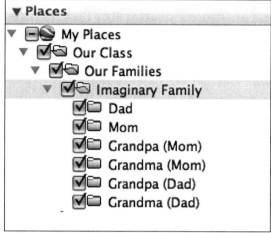

My Places folders

Did You Know? ⊗

There are many genealogy websites available that can trace families back hundreds of years, and link families to famous people or places in history.

Name _____ Date _____

Back in Time

  Choose an imaginary character and fill in the family tree below.

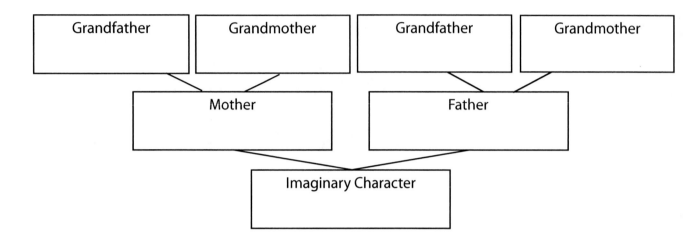

  Fill in the chart with the name of each person and their birthplace. List one major historical event that happened during each person's lifetime.

Name	Birthplace/Year	Major Historical Event

Back in Time *(cont.)*

 3 In the space below, create your own family tree. Fill in your name and the names of your relatives.

Back in Time *(cont.)*

 4   Fill in the chart below with each of your relatives' birthplace, year of birth, and one major historical event from that year. Placemark each location in Google Earth.

Name	Birthplace/Year	Major Historical Event

 5   On a separate sheet of paper, write a one-page story about your family's journeys.

Making Literature Connections

Google Earth Tools

- File: Save: Save Place As...*
- Layers panel: 3D Buildings, Roads*
- Places panel: Folders
- Toolbar: Placemark

Overview

Students will investigate the locations of settings from fictional stories and save locations from literature to the *Our Library* folder and save folders.

Vocabulary

- setting

Materials

- *New York Stories* activity sheets (pages 94–96)

Procedure

1. Tell students that there are many books with settings that they might be able to find in Google Earth. Distribute copies of the *New York Stories* activity sheets (pages 94–96) to students and open Google Earth.

2. Have students read the passage from *From the Mixed Up Files of Mrs. Basil E. Frankweiler* (Konigsburg 1987) on their activity sheets, or read it aloud while students follow along silently. Tell students they will investigate the setting described in this passage.

3. **Fly to** the Metropolitan Muesum of Art, New York, and **placemark** the museum. Create a new folder in your *My Library* folder titled *From the Mixed Up Files of Mrs. Basil E. Frankwweiler*, and add the **placemark** to this folder.

4. In the **Layers panel**, turn on **3D Buildings** and the **Roads layer**. **Zoom** in to the corner of Madison Avenue and 80th Street (one block southeast of the south end of the museum) and use the **navigation tools** to look around and "walk" northwest up 80th Street, then turn northeast (right) on 5th Avenue to the museum. Have students write a description of the museum entrance on their activity sheets (question 1).

* Tool introduced in this lesson

Making Literature Connections *(cont.)*

Procedure *(cont.)*

5 *From the Mixed Up Files of Mrs. Basil E. Frankweiler* is just one of many books that take place in New York City. Tell students that they may work on their own, with partners, or in groups to investigate one of the locations listed on their activity sheets.

6 Assign one location to each student, pair, or group to investigate. Tell students to visit this location in Google Earth, paying attention to as many details as possible. Have students **placemark** their assigned location, create a book folder for the **placemark** using the title of the book, and add the folder to the *Our Library* subfolder in the **My Places panel.** Have them write a description of their assigned setting on their activity sheets (question 2).

7 Have each group show their folders to the class in Google Earth and read their descriptions of the setting aloud.

8 Turn on all the New York book folders and have students look at how far apart the different locations are. Ask students to choose two characters from different books and tell where they might have "bumped into" each other if they were real and lived at the same time (question 3).

9 Save your *Our Library* folder as a backup. Highlight it in the **Places panel**. Select **File** in the

Menu Bar, then **Save**, and **Save Place As...**. A pop-up window will appear, asking you where you want to save the folder and what you want to call it. The saved folder will be a **.kmz file**. Save it on your desktop and name it *library.kmz*.

10 Have students work in groups to create a folder for another book they have read and save their new folder on the desktop. Ask students to write the title of the folder and the location of the placemark on their activity sheets (question 4). Then have students share their folder with the class by double-clicking on the **.kmz file** on the desktop.

11 On their activity sheets, have students write a description of what they see in Google Earth at their chosen location and compare it to what they thought the setting looked like when they read the book (question 5).

Extension Activities

- Have students sort other books they have read by **placemarking** the different locations and creating subfolders.
- Have students investigate settings from nonfiction books and create more **placemarks**.

Making Literature Connections *(cont.)*

Did You Know?

If you can send emails to your students, you can attach the *library.kmz* file as a means of sharing your class work. When students receive the email they should click on the attached file and it will open in Google Earth. The library folder will be in the Temporary Places folder in the Places panel.

Screenshot

New York story setting placemarks

Name _____ Date _____

New York Stories

Directions: Read the excerpt below. Then, answer the questions that follow.

Excerpt from *From the Mixed-up Files of Mrs. Basil E. Frankweiler* (Koningsburg 1987)

> "...Claudia instructed Jamie to wait for her on the corner of Madison Avenue and 80th Street, for there they would turn left onto Fifth Avenue.
>
> She found Jamie standing on that corner, probably one of the most civilized street corners in the whole world, consulting a compass and announcing that when they turned left, they would be heading 'due northwest.'" (page 34)

1 Follow Jamie and Claudia's route from the corner of Madison Avenue and 80th street northwest to Fifth Avenue and then northeast to the Metropolitan Museum of Art. Describe the entrance to the museum.

_____

_____

_____

_____

_____

_____

New York Stories *(cont.)*

 2 Fly to one New York location from the list of fiction books below. Use the navigation tools to investigate the location and the area surrounding it.

- *Stuart Little* (White 1974): Central Park Boathouse, where Stuart sails
- *Eloise* (Thompson 1969): The Plaza, the hotel where Eloise lives
- *The Dinosaurs of Waterhouse Hawkins* (Selznick 2001): Central Park, where the dinosaurs may be buried
- *Harriet the Spy* (Fitzhugh 2001): Carl Schurz Park, where Harriet and her friends play

Write a description of the location you visited in Google Earth:

_____

_____

_____

_____

_____

_____

3 Choose two New York characters from the books your class investigated. Where would they be most likely to meet if they were real and lived at the same time?

_____

_____

_____

_____

New York Stories *(cont.)*

4 Choose another book you have read and find a location from the story in Google Earth. Placemark the location, add it to your library folder, and save it on the desktop. Write the name of the folder and the location of the placemark:

Folder Name: _____

Placemark Location: _____

5 Write a description of the setting as you see it in Google Earth. How is it different from what you imagined it looked like when you read the book?

_____

_____

_____

_____

_____

_____

_____

_____

_____

_____

Building History Connections

Google Earth Tools

- Status bar: Eye alt
- Toolbar: Placemark

Overview

Students will add information to their *My Studies* folders by following the route of Columbus.

Vocabulary

- horizon
- setting

Materials

- *A Path Through History* activity sheets (pages 100–102)
- *Columbus* (Parin D'Aulaire 1992) or other related book (optional)
- tape measure

Procedure

1 Ask students to recall the journey of Christopher Columbus. Distribute copies of *A Path Through History* activity sheets (pages 100–102) to students. Read aloud a portion of *Columbus* (Parin D'Aulaire 1992) or a passage from another book describing Columbus's journey.

2 Have students look at the photo of the replica of the Pinta on their activity sheets and read the statistics about this ship. To help students get a sense of the size of the ship, use a tape measure to determine the length and width of your classroom and have students record these measurements on their activity sheets (question 1). Have students compare the size of your classroom to the size of the Pinta and predict how many men could live on the ship (question 2). Tell students that 26 men crewed the Pinta when it sailed with Columbus.

3 Open Google Earth and **placemark** the following locations from Columbus's journey:

- Palos, Spain
- Canary Islands, Spain
- San Salvador, Bahamas
- Cuba
- Haiti (formerly Hispanola)

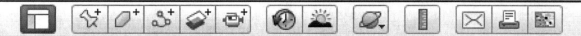

Building History Connections (cont.)

Procedure (cont.)

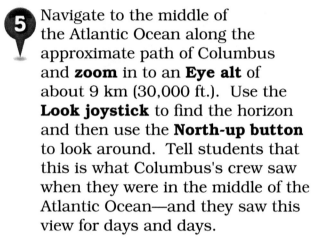

4 Have students write a brief description of the features they see at each location (question 3).

5 Navigate to the middle of the Atlantic Ocean along the approximate path of Columbus and **zoom** in to an **Eye alt** of about 9 km (30,000 ft.). Use the **Look joystick** to find the horizon and then use the **North-up button** to look around. Tell students that this is what Columbus's crew saw when they were in the middle of the Atlantic Ocean—and they saw this view for days and days.

6 Ask students to write a creative journal entry on their activity sheets from the perspective of one of the sailors describing life aboard this ship on this long journey (question 4).

Extension Activities

- Columbus's second, third, and fourth journeys can also be **placemarked**. Save the **placemarks** from each journey in separate subfolders in their *Our Studies* folder in Google Earth.

- Think of holidays that are associated with specific locations (e.g., Arlington Cemetery, Virginia for Memorial Day; Mt. Vernon, Washington for President's Day; the Lincoln Memorial, Washington, DC for Martin Luther King Jr. Day). Have students investigate those locations and **placemark** them in Google Earth, then create a *Holidays* folder to save them. Encourage students to include holidays from other countries, too.

Did You Know?

The first recorded landing of Europeans in North America was by Leif Erikson in 1,000 A.D. Norse stories suggest Erikson landed on Baffin Island and then sailed along the Labrador Coast of Canada, eventually settling in Newfoundland.

Building History Connections *(cont.)*

User Tips

If you want to print an image from Google Earth, click the **Print tool** in the **Toolbar**. Select **Graphic of 3D View** and then **Screen**, **Low**, or **Medium**, depending on how high you would like the resolution of your print. Then select **Print**. (**Note:** The dimensions listed after each print option will vary depending on how your **Google Earth Window** is adjusted.)

If you have difficulty locating a historic site, the National Park Service can often help. On the Internet, go to http://www.nps.gov and click on *Find a Park*. Type in the name of the historic place. Look around the website for directions or a map that can help you locate the site. If you used the National Park Service's website to help you locate an area, include a reference to it on any display.

Screenshot

Columbus's stops in the Caribbean

Name _____ Date _____

A Path Through History

Directions: Read the description below and then answer the questions that follow.

The Pinta was smaller than the Santa María, weighing approximately 60 tons with a length of 20 m (66 ft.) and a width of 7 m (23 ft.). The Captain of the Pinta was Martín Alonso Pinzón. Look at the picture of a replica of the Pinta below.

1 What are the measurements of your classroom?

Length: _____

Width: _____

2 Compare the size of the Pinta to the size of your classroom. How many men do you think could live comfortably on the ship for months at a time?

_____

The actual size of the crew: _____

A Path Through History *(cont.)*

3 Write the name of each location you placemarked on Columbus's journey and write a brief description of the features you see there in the chart.

Location	Description

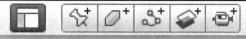

A Path Through History *(cont.)*

4 Pretend you are a sailor on the Pinta. Write a journal entry describing your journey and some of the locations you have visited.

_____

_____

_____

_____

_____

_____

_____

_____

_____

_____

_____

_____

_____

_____

_____

_____

_____

_____

Mapping the Plot of a Book

Google Earth Tools

- Layers: Borders and Labels
- Status bar: Eye alt
- Toolbar: Placemark with Description and View*
- Toolbar: Ruler

Overview

Students will learn that settings of books often take place in real locations, and that these settings can be mapped using Google Earth as a means of further understanding a story.

Vocabulary

- barren
- kelp

Materials

- *Customizing Placemarks* activity sheets (pages 106–108)

* Tool introduced in this lesson

Procedure

1 Distribute copies of the *Customizing Placemarks* activity sheets (pages 106–108) to students and open Google Earth. Have students read Excerpt 1 from *Island of the Blue Dolphins* (O'Dell 1960) on their activity sheets.

2 Karana's island is San Nicolas Island, California. **Fly to** this island and **placemark** it at an **Eye alt** of about 13 km (42,000 ft.). File the **placemark** in a new folder called *Island of the Blue Dolphins* and add it to your *Our Library* folder. On their activity sheets, have students read the first passage and write the comparison the author makes to the shape of the island (question 1).

3 Have students read the second passage and ask students if the island looks barren to them. Do students see any trees? Crops? Green grasslands? Have them write their answers on their activity sheets (question 2).

4 Right-click on the San Nicolas Island **placemark** in the **Places panel**, and select **Get Info** (Mac) or **Properties** (PC). Click on the **View tab** to see or add information about the view currently in the **3D viewer**. Use the **navigation tools** to select a view that emphasizes how barren the island is and click **Snapshot current view**. Close the **Placemark window**. When you open the **placemark** again, the new view will appear in the **3D viewer**.

Mapping the Plot of a Book *(cont.)*

Procedure *(cont.)*

5 The **Placemark window** includes a **Description tab**. Ask students to write a sentence on their activity sheets in the sample **Placemark window** (question 3) that describes the vegetation of San Nicolas. How was Karana able to eat? Ask several students to share their descriptions and enter one in the **Placemark window**.

6 While Karana is on her island, the Aleuts come and hunt sea otter in the kelp. **Zoom** in to the waters surrounding the island (**Eye alt** about 305 m or 1,000 ft.) and look for the kelp beds. (They look like brown blotches in the water about a half-mile from shore.) **Placemark** one of the kelp beds and ask students to choose a quote from their activity sheets (question 4) to add to the **Placemark window**.

7 Karana is stranded on the island for many years. Although she has a canoe, her attempt to row to Santa Catalina Island fails. Navigate to San Nicolas Island at an **Eye alt** of about 320 km (200 mi.) to emphasize its location relative to other islands in the region and the coast of California.

8 Turn on the **Borders and Labels layer** and **placemark** Santa Catalina Island. Ask students to mark it on the map on their activity sheets (question 5).

9 Use the **ruler tool** to determine the distance between San Nicolas and Santa Catalina, and add a description to the Santa Catalina **placemark** that describes how far Karana would have had to row to get there. Have students write this distance on their activity sheets and answer the questions that follow (questions 6 and 7).

Extension Activities

- Ships could anchor in Coral Cove and smaller boats could then carry people to the shore. Navigate around the island and look for a cove that may have been Coral Cove. Choose a passage from the book that describes the cove. Create a **placemark** and add the quote to the **Placemark window**.

- Karana was constantly looking for a ship from Santa Barbara to rescue her and watching out for the Aleutians' ship, which she feared. **Placemark** the Aleutian Islands with a view that shows the entire chain of islands. Add a description to the **placemark** that describes the route the Aleuts took to get to Karana's island in the **Placemark window** and move the **placemark** to your I*sland of the Blue Dolphins* folder.

Mapping the Plot of a Book *(cont.)*

Did You Know? ✕

San Nicolas Island was originally inhabited by the Nicoleño people. In various conflicts, Aleutian trappers killed many Nicoleños. The Nicoleños were removed by the padres of the California missions in the early 19th century. Karana was based on "The Lone Woman of San Nicolas Island," a woman who was left on the island for 18 years when her people were removed. She was eventually rescued and taken to the mission in Santa Barbara where she died within weeks. Today, the island is a Navy base with about 200 Navy personnel and a small airport.

Screenshot

DATA LDEO—COLUMBIA, NSF, NOAA, IMAGE U.S. GEOLOGICAL SURVEY,
DATA SIO, NOAA, U.S. NAVY, NGA, GEBCO

The Channel Islands of California

Name _____ Date _____

Customizing Placemarks

Directions: Read the passages below. Then answer the questions that follow.

> Excerpt 1 from *Island of the Blue Dolphins* (O'Dell 1960)
>
> "Our island is two leagues long and one league wide, and if you were standing on one of the hills that rise in the middle of it, you would think that it looked like a fish. Like a dolphin lying on its side, with its tail pointing toward the sunrise, its nose pointing to the sunset, and its fins making the reefs and the rocky ledges along the shore."

 What shape did the author compare the island to?

_____

Do you agree or disagree with the author?

_____

> Excerpt 2 from *Island of the Blue Dolphins* (O'Dell 1960)
>
> "All the winds except the one from the south are strong, and because of them the hills are polished smooth and the trees are small and twisted, even in the canyon that runs down to Coral Cove."

 Does the island look barren? Describe what you see.

_____

_____

_____

Customizing Placemarks *(cont.)*

 3 In the Description box below, write a sentence that describes the vegetation on the island and explain how Karana was able to find food.

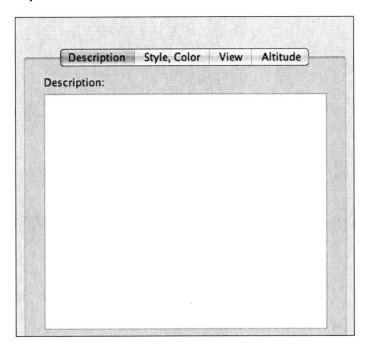

 4 Choose one of the quotes from *Island of the Blue Dolphins* below that best describes the kelp and circle it.

- "The wide beds of kelp which surround our island on three sides come close to shore and spread out to sea for a distance of a league."

- "The otter likes to lie on its back in the kelp beds, floating up and down to the motion of the waves, sunning itself or sleeping."

- "From the cliff I could see the skin canoes darting here and there over the kelp beds, barely skimming the water, and the long spears flying like arrows."

Customizing Placemarks *(cont.)*

 5   Mark San Nicolas Island and Santa Catalina Island on the image below.

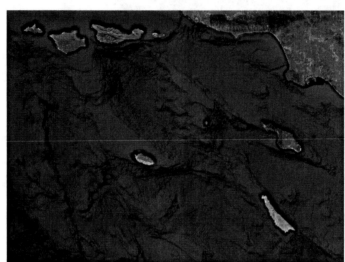

DATA LDEO–COLUMBIA, NSF, NOAA, IMAGE U.S. GEOLOGICAL SURVEY, DATA SIO, NOAA, U.S. NAVY, NGA, GEBCO

6   In Google Earth, use the ruler tool to measure the distance from San Nicolas Island to Santa Catalina Island. What is the distance?

_____

 7   Do you think Karana could easily row from her island to another island or to the mainland? Why or why not?

_____

_____

_____

_____

_____

Following the Path of a Book

Standards

Students know the ways in which changes in people's perceptions of environments have influenced human migration and settlement over time.

Students make, confirm, and revise simple predictions about what will be found in a text.

Google Earth Tools

- Toolbar: Placemark
- Toolbar: Path*

Overview

Students will learn to follow a path taken by characters in a book and that the path can be mapped using Google Earth as a means of further understanding the setting of a story.

Vocabulary

- plot

Materials

- *Tracing a Journey* activity sheets (pages 112–114)
- *By the Great Horn Spoon!* (Fleischman 1965)

Procedure

1 Distribute copies of the *Tracing a Journey* activity sheets (pages 112–114) to students and open Google Earth. Review the plot of the book *By the Great Horn Spoon!* (Fleischman 1965) with students.

2 Read the five excerpts on the activity sheet that denote the major stops on Jack's journey from Boston to San Francisco (question 1) and navigate to the general area of each location (e.g., North America, South America). Once in the general area of the Earth, **Fly to** each respective location and **zoom** in. Look for ships in each present-day harbor to find where Jack may have anchored. **Placemark** each major stop on Jack's journey.

3 File the **placemarks** in a new subfolder under *Our Library* called *By the Great Horn Spoon!*

4 To trace Jack's journey from Boston to San Francisco, it is helpful to draw a **path** to illustrate the sequence of events. Look for the **Path tool** in the **Toolbar**.

* Tool introduced in this lesson

Following the Path of a Book *(cont.)*

Procedure *(cont.)*

5 **Zoom** out to a view that includes both Boston and Rio de Janeiro (**Eye alt** about 9,600 km or 6,000 mi.). Click once on the **path tool** in the **Toolbar**. The cursor will turn to a square, and a **Path window** will appear. Name the **path** *Lady Wilma's Journey*. Do not click **OK** until the **path** is complete. To make the **path**, place the cursor over the Boston **placemark** and click to start the **path**. (*Note:* When building a **path**, use the **navigation tools** to move the Earth, not your mouse.) Move the cursor out to the Atlantic Ocean and click again. You will see a line connecting the two dots.

6 Continue making the **path** from Boston to Rio de Janeiro by clicking on the thumbtacks in the **3D viewer** in the order traveled in the book, then click **OK** to close the **Path window**. A folder titled *Lady Wilma's Journey* will appear at the bottom of the **Places panel**. Drag the **Path folder** to the *By the Great Horn Spoon* folder. Have students answer questions 2 and 3 on their activity sheets about the temperatures Jack may have encountered on his journey and whether he crossed the Equator.

7 The Lady Wilma passed through the Strait of Magellan, so you need to add that to your path. Right-click on the *Lady Wilma's Journey* folder and select **Get Info** (Mac) or **Properties** (PC) to open the **Path window**. Use the **navigation tools** to rotate the Earth so both the Strait of Magellan and Rio de Janeiro are in view.

8 Click on the last point of the path at Rio de Janeiro to select it. You can now add new points to illustrate the journey through the Strait of Magellan, up the coast of Chile, to the Galapagos, and on to San Francisco (it is not important to follow the strait in detail).

9 Click on the **Measurements tab** in the **Path window** and ask students to write the distance of the path on their activity sheets in miles (question 4). Praiseworthy said they would travel 15,000 miles. Was he right?

10 On their activity sheets, have students write a postcard from Jack describing his journey (question 5).

Following the Path of a Book *(cont.)*

Extension Activities

- Gold seekers often traveled from the east coast to San Francisco the way Jack did. Others traveled over land and still others traveled to Panama, then over land, and then continued by boat. Use the **path tool** to compare the distances of these three routes.

- Compare the *By the Great Horn Spoon!* **path** and *The Island of the Blue Dolphins* **placemarks**. Could Karana and Jack have crossed paths or seen each other? Remind students that Karana lived alone on San Nicolas Island from 1835 until 1853, and Jack traveled to the gold rush in 1849.

Did You Know?

The Panama Canal joins the Atlantic Ocean and the Pacific Ocean. It was built between 1904 and 1914. It replaced the long and treacherous routes through the Strait of Magellan and around Cape Horn, cutting the distance between New York and San Francisco in half.

User Tip

When the **Path window** is open, you will need to navigate using the **Move joystick** and **zoom slider**. Using the cursor will alter your path. If you do this accidentally, you can erase the last point on a path by right-clicking (or control-clicking) on it.

Screenshots

Path tool

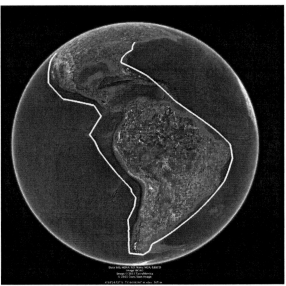

DATA SIO, NOAA, U.S. NAVY, NGA, GEBCO, IMAGE IBCAO, IMAGE © 2011 TARRAMETRICS, © 2011 CNES/SPOT IMAGE

By The Great Horn Spoon! path

Name _____ Date _____

Tracing a Journey

1 Find each of the following locations from *By the Great Horn Spoon!* (Fleischman 1965) and create a placemark for it in Google Earth:

- **Boston, Massachusetts**: "A sailing ship with two great sidewheels went splashing out of Boston harbor on a voyage around the Horn to San Francisco."

- **Rio de Janeiro, Brazil**: "With the coming of dawn the sidewheeler entered the channel and passed under the fortress guns of Rio de Janeiro."

- **Strait of Magellan** (53 28 51 S 70 47 00 W): "Dark cliffs seemed to hang like draperies from the misty sky…"

- **Coquimbo, Chile**: "Day after day the two gold ships beat their way north along the ragged coast of Chile."

- **Galapagos Islands, Ecuador**: "Hoping for a supply of coal, Captain Swain dropped anchor in the Galapagos. But there was nothing to be had except a few cords of stove wood on those barren islands."

- **San Francisco, California**: "By noon the Golden Gate stood ahead of them."

2 Look at your path. Did Jack cross the Equator? How do you know?

_____

_____

_____

_____

Tracing a Journey *(cont.)*

3 As Jack traveled from Boston to Rio de Janeiro, he encountered some changes in temperature. Write how you think the temperature changed during the journey.

_____

_____

_____

_____

4 Read the passage below. Then answer the questions that follow.

> Excerpt from *By the Great Horn Spoon!* (Fleischman 1965)
>
> "'If I may observe,' Praiseworthy remarked with his perfect calm, 'It is a fifteen-thousand-mile voyage around Cape Horn to San Francisco, I believe. It is not the beginning of a race that counts, sir, but the end.'"

Look at the Measurements tab in the Edit Path window. Write the distance of the path you have created. Praiseworthy said they would travel 15,000 miles. Was Praiseworthy's prediction correct? How do you know?

_____

_____

_____

_____

Tracing a Journey *(cont.)*

 5 Jack landed at Long Wharf in San Francisco. Describe how Jack might have felt after traveling so far. Pretend you are Jack. Write a postcard home to Boston describing your journey.

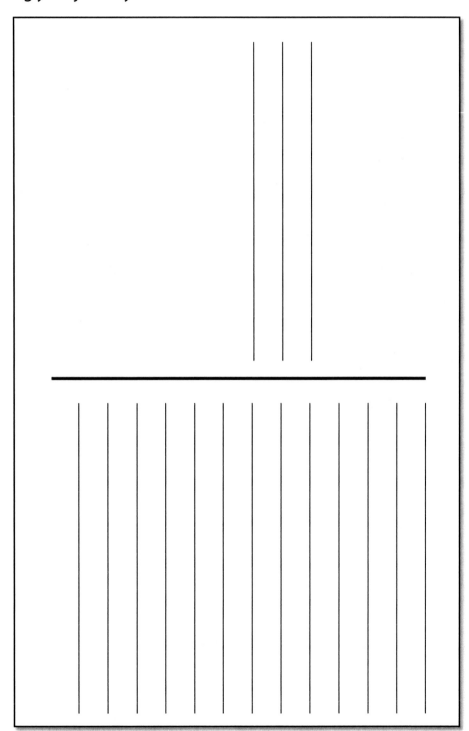

Touring a Book

Google Earth Tools

- Toolbar: Placemark
- Toolbar: Tour*

Overview

Students will create a tour of the settings of a book as a means of summarizing a story.

Vocabulary

- journey
- timeline

Materials

- *Take Me There* activity sheets (pages 118–120)
- *By the Great Horn Spoon!* (Fleischman 1965) or another reading book

Procedure

1 In the last lesson, students gained a two-dimensional perspective for the setting of *By the Great Horn Spoon!* (Fleischman 1965) by drawing a path to illustrate Jack's journey. To get a better idea of the variety of ports that Jack visited, make a **tour** of the journey. Distribute copies of the *Take Me There* activity sheets (pages 118–120) to students and open Google Earth.

2 Tell students that when they have several places that tell a story, they can make a **tour** of the locations in Google Earth by using their **placemarks**. Tell students to fill in the timeline of the story on their activity sheets (question 1). Put the **placemarks** in your *By the Great Horn Spoon!* folder into chronological order by dragging and dropping them.

3 Click on the **tour tool** in the **Toolbar**. A **record-tour panel** will appear in the lower-left corner of the **3D viewer**. The red button on the left is the **start/stop button**. The numbers indicate the duration of the **tour** in minutes and seconds (mm:ss).

* Tool introduced in this lesson

Touring a Book *(cont.)*

Procedure *(cont.)*

4 Double-click on the first **placemark** in the *By the Great Horn Spoon!* folder. The **3D viewer** will navigate to the location of this **placemark**. To start a **tour,** click the **start/ stop button**. The entire button will turn red. Wait a second and then double-click on the second **placemark**. The **3D viewer** will then navigate to this **placemark**. Double-click the third **placemark** and the **3D viewer** will navigate to this place. Continue to the last **placemark**, then click the **start/stop button** to stop the **tour**.

5 A **play-tour panel** will appear and the **tour** will automatically start playing. The **play-tour panel** includes (from the left) **go back, play**, and **fast forward buttons**, a **tour slider**, an indicator of the **current time** of the **tour**, a **repeat button,** and a **save button**.

6 Click the **save button** to save the **tour**. Give the **tour** a title, and then click **OK**. Move the **tour** folder to the *By the Great Horn Spoon!* folder.

7 Play the **tour** again by double-clicking on the **tour** folder. As the **tour** is playing, have students make notes on how they would improve the **tour** (question 2).

8 Record a new **tour** including students' suggested improvements, and play it for the class. Have students choose another book with a real-life setting and plan a Google Earth tour for it (question 3).

Extension Activity

Create a tour of your city, region, or state and play it for parents on Open House or Parents' Night.

Did You Know?

There are many tours available online. Look at some tours to get an idea about some ways to customize your tours even further.

User Tip

Always close the **record-** and **play-tour panels** when you are finished using them because many other tools are disabled while the **record-** or **play-tour** panels are open.

Touring a Book *(cont.)*

Screenshots

Tour tool

record-tour panel

play-tour panel

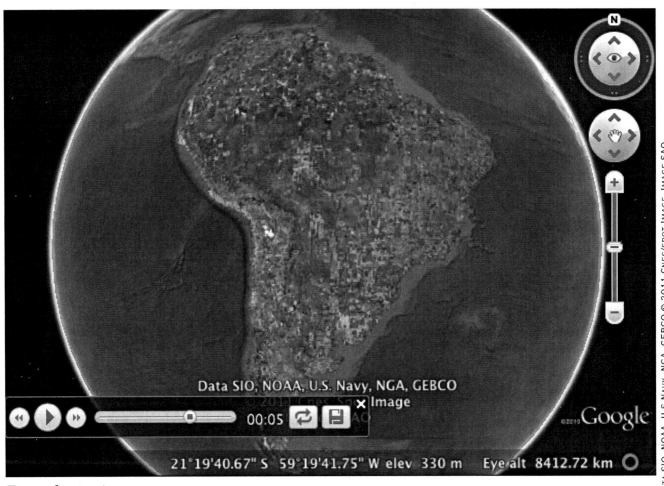

Recording a tour

Name _____ Date _____

Take Me There

 On the timeline below, add the events of the story in the order they happened.

├──┤

Take Me There *(cont.)*

2 As you watch the tour, make notes about how you could make it better.

_____

_____

_____

_____

_____

_____

_____

_____

_____

_____

_____

_____

Take Me There *(cont.)*

3 Make a plan to create a tour of another book you are reading, or a tour of a significant event or location in history. In the storyboard boxes below, sketch the sequence of the tour, and add any details you want to include.

1

Details _____
_____

2

Details _____
_____

4

Details _____
_____

3

Details _____
_____

5

Details _____
_____

6

Details _____
_____

Creating a Book Report

Standards

Students know the ways in which changes in people's perceptions of environments have influenced human migration and settlement over time.

Students make basic oral presentations to the class.

Google Earth Tools

- Toolbar: Placemark: Style, Color*
- Toolbar: Tour: Audio*

Overview

Students will map the path of a book, create a tour of the locations, and add their voice to narrate the tour as a means of creating a book report.

Vocabulary

- narrate

Materials

- *Telling a Story* activity sheets (pages 124–126)
- fiction or nonfiction book with real locations
- Google Earth tour (from the previous lesson)

Procedure

1. Play the **tour** of *By the Great Horn Spoon!* (Fleischman 1965) from the previous lesson. Ask students to review what they see in the **tour**. Distribute copies of the *Telling a Story* activity sheets (pages 124–126) to students and open Google Earth.

2. List the **placemarks** that make up the **tour** on the board. Have students list them on their activity sheets (question 1).

3. Have students choose three key locations that they want to describe in detail. Have students write brief descriptions of their three chosen locations (question 2). Descriptions should include why the location is significant to the story, features seen in Google Earth, and any other details that are important to the story.

4. To turn the **tour** into a book report, tell students they will add a title, an ending, and narration to their **tour** in Google Earth.

* Tool introduced in this lesson

Creating a Book Report *(cont.)*

Procedure *(cont.)*

5 Have students select a **placemark** to be the start of the **tour**, and another **placemark** to be the end. (For example, in *By the Great Horn Spoon!*, the **tour** would start in Boston and end in San Francisco.)

6 Show students how to change the name of the first **placemark by** right-clicking on the **placemark** and selecting **Get Info** (Mac) or **Properties** (PC) to open the **Placemark window**. Change the name in the **Name box** to a title for the tour. The name could be simply the title of the book. Choose a large, colorful font using the **Style, Color tab** in the **Placemark window**.

7 Change the name of the last **placemark** to *The End.* Again, choose a large colorful font.

8 On their activity sheets, have students work individually or in small groups to prepare a script of what they will say at each **placemark** as the tour is playing (question 3).

9 Have students rehearse with a partner or group before recording their narrations directly to the **tour**. Students should time each other and try to keep their recording under five minutes.

10 To record students' voices, click on the **microphone button** in the **record-tour panel** and have them read aloud into the microphone on the computer. Have each student or group of students record audio for the tour, and then play it back for the class.

Creating a Book Report *(cont.)*

Extension Activity

Have students create a **tour** using the locations they discovered in the lesson on *Follwing Our Family Trees* (pages 85–90). Tell them to use the **microphone button** to record a narration, including songs, poems, or stories, and have students play their **tours** for their families.

User Tip

You can stop a **tour** to look around by clicking on the **pause button**, or by pressing the space bar.

Screenshot

record-tour panel

Did You Know?

It is possible to add pictures and even embed video clips into a **tour**. However, doing so will significantly increase the file storage size of the **tour**. Check your Internet connection speed and broadband capability before embedding pictures or videos.

Name _____ Date _____

Telling a Story

1 Write the title of your book below, and list the placemarks that make up your tour.

Book: _____

Placemarks

1. _____

2. _____

3. _____

4. _____

5. _____

6. _____

Telling a Story *(cont.)*

 2 Choose three significant locations and write a brief description of each. Include why the location is significant to the story, features you see in Google Earth, and any other details that are important to the story.

Placemark	Description
1.	
2.	
3.	

Telling a Story *(cont.)*

3 Work with a partner and write a script for your tour. Use the placemarks from the previous page to help you plan your tour.

_____

_____

_____

_____

_____

_____

_____

_____

_____

_____

_____

_____

_____

_____

_____

_____

_____

_____

_____

_____

Going Back in Time

Standards
Students know the ways people alter the physical environment. Students know about life in urban areas and communities of various cultures of the world at various times in their history.

Google Earth Tools

- Toolbar: Clock*

Overview

Students will use Google Earth to look back in recent time to discover how baseball fields and the site of the World Trade Center in New York have changed.

Vocabulary

- construction
- demolish
- decade

Materials

- *Times Will Change* activity sheets (pages 130–132)
- 10 sheets of paper
- tape
- markers or colored pencils
- *Ballpark: The Story of America's Baseball Fields* (Curlee 2005) or another book about baseball (optional)
- books about the events of September 11, 2001 (optional)

Procedure

Note: Before beginning this lesson, have students help create a 10-decade timeline by taping ten pieces of paper together lengthwise. Mark one decade per sheet (1920–1930, 1930–1940, 1940–1950, 1950–1960, 1960–1970, 1970–1980, 1980–1990, 1990–2000, 2000–2010, 2010–2020), with the oldest decade on the left and the most recent on the right. Hang the timeline in front of the class.

1 Baseball has been a favorite American pastime for many decades. Read a few pages or show some pictures from *Ballpark: The Story of America's Baseball Fields* (Curlee 2005), or another book about baseball. Ask students how long baseball has been around. Distribute copies of the *Times Will Change* activity sheets (pages 130–132) to students and open Google Earth.

2 Point out the 10-decade timeline you have hung up, and have students refer to the one on their activity sheets. Add the dates listed on the activity sheets to the class timeline, and ask students to add these dates to the timeline on their activity sheets (question 1). Tell students to use different colored pencils to fill in the dates.

* Tool introduced in this lesson

Going Back in Time *(cont.)*

Procedure *(cont.)*

3 **Fly to** Yankee Stadium, New York. Adjust the view to show both the present Yankee Stadium and the field to the southwest that once held the old Yankee Stadium. On their activity sheets, ask students to describe what they see (question 2).

4 Click on the **clock tool** in the **Toolbar**. Point out the **timeline slider** in the upper-left corner of the **3D viewer.** Explain that each vertical bar represents an image that was taken at a different time. (***Note:*** Be sure that the **3D Buildings layer** is turned off in the **Layers panel**.)

5 Use the cursor to move the marker to the left on the **timeline slider** back in time to 1995. On the lines next to "1995" on their activity sheets, ask students to describe what they see (question 2). Explain to students that the 1995 image is of the original Yankee Stadium that was built in 1923.

6 Move the **timeline slider** slowly to the right (forward in time) to watch what happens to Yankee Stadium. Ask students to write down the year construction started on the new stadium, and the year that the old stadium was demolished on their activity sheets (question 3) and to add these dates to their timelines. Have students answer questions 4 and 5 as well. Turn the **clock tool** by clicking it again in the **Toolbar**.

7 Other areas of New York City have also changed. **Fly to** the World Trade Center, New York City, New York. Remind students that on September 11, 2001 the Twin Towers of the World Trade Center were destroyed by terrorists. If desired, read one of the books about September 11, 2001 from the Recommended Literature list (Appendix F).

8 Click the **clock tool** and move the **timeline slider** back to a date before September 11, 2001. Then go forward in time and ask students to describe what they see at this site now (question 6). Encourage students to look carefully. Because the Twin Towers were so tall, there are many large shadows. The buildings look different depending on which side the satellite was on when it took the picture. Have students add the September 11, 2001 date to their timelines.

Going Back in Time *(cont.)*

Extension Activities

- Ask students to write a newspaper article describing a changing structure. Some possible buildings to use include Birds Nest National Stadium, Beijing, China (built for the 2008 Olympic games); Burj Khalifa, Dubai, United Arab Emirates; or the Soccer City Stadium in Johannesburg, South Africa (built for the World Cup).

- **Fly to** these ballparks and view how they have changed over time using the **clock tool**:
  - ➤ Kingdome, Qwest, and Safeco Fields, Seattle, Washington
  - ➤ Reliant Park, Astrodome, and Minute Maid Park, Houston, Texas

Screenshots

Clock tool

Timeline slider

Did You Know?

Explain to students that older pictures are fuzzier because the resolution and image quality of older cameras and instruments was not as good as it is today, and, before the time of satellites, the airplanes on which the older photographs flew to take the pictures were not as stable for picture-taking.

Name _____ Date _____

Times Will Change

 1 Write the letter for each event in the correct place on the timeline below.

    a. The year you were born: _____

    b. The year your school was built: _____

    c. The first Yankee Stadium was built: 1923

    d. The new Yankee Stadium was built: 2009

    e. Little League was founded: 1939

    f. Girls were first allowed to play Little League: 1973

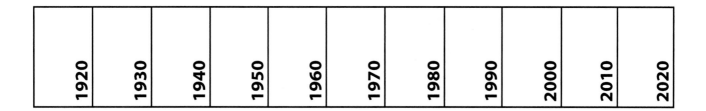

1920	1930	1940	1950	1960	1970	1980	1990	2000	2010	2020

Times Will Change *(cont.)*

2 On the lines below, describe Yankee Stadium as it looks today and as it looked in 1995.

Today: _____

_____

_____

1995: _____

_____

_____

3 In what year was the old stadium demolished? _____

In what year was the new stadium completed? _____

4 Next to each player below, write either *New* or *Old* to indicate in which stadium each player would have played. On the timeline on the previous page, circle the date that each stadium was built to help you answer this question.

_____ Babe Ruth 1914 –1935   _____ Jackie Robinson 1947–1956

_____ Mickey Mantle 1951–1969   _____ Derek Jeter 1995–present

5 Use the ruler tool to see how far the players would have to hit the ball to make a home run (measure from home plate to the furthest point away in center field). Write the distances below.

Old stadium: Home run = _____

New stadium: Home run = _____

Times Will Change *(cont.)*

 6　Below is a picture of the World Trade Center before the events of September 11, 2001. Describe what you see at the site of the World Trade Center today in Google Earth.

_____

_____

_____

_____

_____

_____

_____

Following Explorers

Google Earth Tools

- .kmz files*
- Toolbar: Path, Placemark

Overview

Students will explore the geography along the path of Magellan.

Vocabulary

- archipelago
- inlet
- island
- strait

Materials

- *Magellan's Journey* activity sheets (pages 136–138)
- map of the Straits of Magellan (optional)
- *Who Was Ferdinand Magellan?* (Kramer 2004) (optional)

Procedure

1 Read a book such as *Who Was Ferdinand Magellan?* (Kramer 2004). Ask students to imagine what early explorers saw as they ventured to uncharted parts of our planet.

2 Distribute copies of the *Magellan's Journey* activity sheets (pages 136–138) to students and open Google Earth. Create a *Magellan* subfolder in your *History* folder. **Placemark** and view the locations listed on students' activity sheets and have students use the Word Bank to describe each location (question 1). Add these **placemarks** to your *Magellan* folder.

3 **Fly to** Lisbon, Portugal (the city where Magellan first saw the ocean) and the Spice Islands (the islands Magellan was aiming to find, also called Maluku Islands). **Placemark** each location and add it to your *Magellan* folder.

4 **Zoom** out. Is it possible to get a view of the Earth that shows both Lisbon and the Spice Islands? Ask students how many miles they think Magellan traveled and how long they think this trip would have taken.

* Tool introduced in this lesson

Following Explorers *(cont.)*

Procedure *(cont.)*

5. In your *Magellan* folder, double-click each **placemark** in order, stopping at each location for a moment or two. As you do, have students answer the questions on their activity sheets about Magellan's journey (questions 2–5).

6. Use the **path tool** to create a path that traces Magellan's journey. Store the **path** in the *Magellan* folder. Turn on the *By the Great Horn Spoon!* **path** and have students compare Jack's journey to Magellan's.

7. Open your Internet browser and search for "Ferdinand Magellan kmz." Select a **.kmz file** that shows Magellan's path. Download the **.kmz file** and it will open in Google Earth. Have students compare this path to the one your class created (questions 6 and 7).

Extension Activities

- Measure the circumference of Earth at the equator using the **path tool**. Magellan traveled about 43,400 miles on his journey. Have students divide the length of Magellan's journey by the circumference of Earth to determine how many times Magellan could have circled Earth if he had traveled in a straight line along the Equator.

- Have students select another explorer (e.g., one of the Vikings, Barents, Drake, Cook) whose voyage was mostly ocean-based. Tell students to look for existing **.kmz files** on the Internet that show the explorer's journey. Then have students create a Ship's Log of the places the explorer stopped on his voyage. Lastly, tell students to create a **tour** to tell the story of the explorer's adventure.

Did You Know? ⊗

Magellan is famous for being the first person to circumnavigate the Earth. But he died before he reached Portugal again. Some of his men did make it back to Portugal to complete the journey.

Following Explorers *(cont.)*

User Tip

Some areas, like the Strait of Magellan, are hard to see because so many images are mosaicked together to create the view. **Zoom** in and navigate to follow the water's path through the strait.

Screenshot

The Strait of Magellan

Name _____ Date _____

Magellan's Journey

Use the Word Bank to help you describe each location in Magellan's ship's log below. Some descriptions may be used more than once.

Word Bank
inlet   island   archipelago   strait   peninsula

Ship's Log

Location	Description
San Lucar de Barrameda, Spain	
Canarias Islands, Spain	
Rio de Janeiro, Brazil	
Rio de la Plata, Uruguay	
Port San Julian, Argentina	
Strait of Magellan	
Puka Puka, Tuamotu	
Guam	
The Philippines	

Magellan's Journey *(cont.)*

2 Did Magellan make it all the way around the world?

_____

3 Did Magellan cross the Equator?

_____

4 What do you think was the hardest part of Magellan's voyage? Why do you think so?

_____

_____

_____

_____

_____

5 Using what you see in Google Earth, describe how an inlet is different from a strait.

_____

_____

_____

_____

Magellan's Journey *(cont.)*

Directions: Answer the questions using the map of the Straits of Magellan below.

 6 On the map below, draw the path you created to show Magellan's journey and the .kmz file path that was downloaded from the Internet.

7 Describe how the two paths are similar and how they are different.

_____

_____

_____

_____

_____

Mapping History

Standards

Students know the factors that have contributed to changing land use in a community. Students understand the people, events, problems, and ideas that were significant in creating the history of their state.

Google Earth Tools

- Layers panel: Borders and Labels
- Layers panel: Gallery: Rumsey Historical Maps*
- Toolbar: Placemark

Overview

Students will use historical maps from the late 1700s and 1800s to explore the 13 original colonies and the history of San Francisco.

Vocabulary

- compass rose
- co-registered

Materials

- *Then and Now* activity sheets (pages 142–144)

Procedure

1 Distribute copies of the *Then and Now* activity sheets (pages 142–144) to students and open Google Earth. Have students complete the timeline on their activity sheets (question 1). **Placemark** these locations, record the dates in by adding descriptions in the **Pacemark windows**, and save the placemarks to your *History* folder.

2 Turn on the **Borders and Labels layer** in the **Layers panel**. **Zoom** in on the eastern United States and point out the 13 original colonies to students. Ask students if they think the current states have the same borders as the 13 original colonies.

3 Go to the **Layers panel**, open the **Gallery layer,** and turn on the **Rumsey Historical Maps layer**. These are historical maps that have been scanned and co-registered, or matched, to the Google Earth globe.

4 **Zoom** in on the eastern United States until yellow **compass rose icons** appear (**Eye alt** 2,700 km or 1,700 mi.). Click once on a **compass rose icon** to see a **Compass Rose Map window** containing a map, a name, and a date. Then, find the **compass rose icon** labeled "North America 1786." (***Note:*** It is near the borders of Kansas, Arkansas, Missouri, and Oklahoma. It may be necessary to **zoom** in to find it.)

* Tool introduced in this lesson

Mapping History *(cont.)*

Procedure *(cont.)*

5 Click once on the map in the **Compass Rose Map window**. The window will disappear and a historical map will appear in the **3D viewer**. **Zoom** out to see the full extent of the map, and then **zoom** in to about 1,900 km (1,200 mi.). Have students find the date of the map on their timeline.

6 Turn the historical map on and off in the **Temporary Places folder** in the **Places panel** to compare America just after the Revolutionary War to America today. (**Note:** The maps are not exactly co-registered, meaning some places on the Rumsey map are not where they should be.) Alternate between the present day view and the historical map, and ask students to name some of the natural features that help determine the borders of states (question 2). Turn off the historical map in the **Layers panel** and **Temporary Places folder**.

7 Tell students there are also historical maps of cities available in Google Earth. **Fly to** San Francisco, California, and look for the **compass rose icon** labeled "San Francisco 1859." Double-click on the **compass rose icon**, and click on the map in the **Compass Rose Map window** to overlay the 1859 historical map on top of present-day San Francisco. Have students find the date of the map on their timeline.

8 Have students write a paragraph comparing San Francisco from 1859 to today, using what they see in Google Earth (question 3).

Extension Activities

- From the **Compass Rose Map window**, you can click **Download links to all Rumsey Historical Maps** to see additional Rumsey maps. Look for the following **compass rose icons** in the Nebraska/South Dakota area: United States 1816; United States 1823; United States 1839; United States 1867. Discuss with students the changes that took place over time and use these maps to help students envision Westward Expansion.

- Click on the "United States 1816" **compass rose icon**. Look for the Mississippi Territory and the Arkansas Territory. Have students make an argument about why these territories should be admitted to the Union. How many states could each territory support, and where would the borders be located? Then, look at the present day states. How closely did students predict the locations of states?

Mapping History *(cont.)*

Did You Know? ✕

David Rumsey is a map collector. Many of his maps have been digitized and added to Google Earth. Additional maps are available on his website: http://www.davidrumsey.com/.

Screenshots

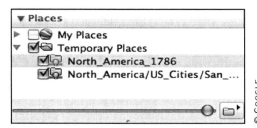

© GOOGLE

Temporary Places folder

Screenshot

San Francisco 1859 Rumsey Historical Map

Name _____ Date _____

Then and Now

 1   Use the information below to fill in the following dates on the timeline on the next page.

1607   Jamestown Colony is established in present-day Virginia

1775   Paul Revere begins his ride in Boston, Massachusetts

1776   Declaration of Independence is signed in Philadelphia, Pennsylvania

1804   Lewis and Clark begin their expedition in Saint Charles, Missouri

1846   The Oregon Trail is in full swing

1607   Virginia becomes the first colony

1787   Delaware becomes the first state

1790   Rhode Island is the last colony to become a state

Then and Now *(cont.)*

Jamestown Colony is established: 1607 ———

1600
1610
1620
1630
1640
1650
1660
1670
1680
1690
1700
1710
1720
1730
1740
1750
1760
1770
1780
1790
1800
1810
1820
1830
1840
1850

Then and Now *(cont.)*

Directions: Use the information from the timeline to answer the questions below.

2 While comparing the old maps of the colonies with today's map of the United States, name three natural features that helped determine the borders of states.

_____

_____

_____

3 Write a paragraph describing how San Francisco looked in 1859, and compare it to how it looks today using what you discovered from the historical map.

_____

_____

_____

_____

_____

_____

_____

_____

_____

_____

_____

_____

_____

_____

_____

Tracking the News

Standards

Students know natural hazards that occur in the physical environment. Students know how to interpret data presented in timelines (e.g., identify the time at which events occurred; the sequence in which events developed; what else was occurring at the time).

Google Earth Tools

- Layers panel: Gallery: Earthquakes*
- Status bar: Eye alt
- Toolbar: Clock

Overview

Students will investigate current events and explore the effects of earthquakes.

Vocabulary

- intensity

Materials

- *Earthquake Strikes!* activity sheets (pages 149–150)
- Website: http://www.earthquake.usgs.gov
- *TIME® for Kids* or another news magazine (optional)

Procedure

1 Talk with students about what has been happening in the news and where in the world these events are happening. Show students some pictures from *TIME® for Kids* or another news magazine and ask students to identify some news events for which a location is important. Distribute copies of the *Earthquake Strikes!* activity sheets (pages 149–150) to students and open your Internet browser.

2 Over the last several years a lot of newsworthy changes have happened on Earth. Earthquakes of great intensity, or exceptionally great force, have struck various regions around the world. As news events happen, Google Earth tries to obtain the most recent imagery and post it in Google Earth.

3 Open your Internet browser and go to http://www.gearthblog.com. Scroll down the page to see a variety of newsworthy events. Choose one, read about it, and click on the **KML** link (usually in the text) to see the event in Google Earth.

* Tool introduced in this lesson

Tracking the News *(cont.)*

Procedure *(cont.)*

Tell students that they are going to observe another major event in Google Earth, the earthquake that struck Haiti on January 12, 2010. **Fly to** Port-au-Prince, Haiti. **Zoom** in to the Presidential Palace (18 32 35 N 72 20 20 W at an **Eye alt** of about 460 m or 1,500 ft.), and use the **clock tool** to set the **timeline slider** to August 25, 2009. Ask students to describe what they see on their activity sheets (question 1).

Move the **timeline slider** ahead to January 16, 2010 (four days after the earthquake). Ask students to describe what they see now on their activity sheets (question 2). Have them look to the north, east, and west of the palace, and **zoom** in to get a closer look. Although it is not possible to see a fault line, it is possible to see the rubble in the streets.

6 Move the **timeline slider** ahead to the mark at November 8, 2010. Ask students to describe what they see now on their activity sheets (question 3). **Zoom** out and look at the blue and white tent cities that were set up as temporary housing for the people who lost their homes in the earthquake. Use the **clock tool** to go backwards and forward, and estimate how long people lived in this "temporary housing" (question 4). Ask students to find more evidence of temporary housing in the city.

7 Go to the **Layers panel** and open the **Gallery layer** and then turn on the **Earthquakes layer**.

8 Keeping Port-au-Prince centered in the **3D viewer**, **zoom** out to an **Eye alt** of about 37 km (23 mi.). Navigate so that Port-au-Prince is in the upper-right corner of the **3D viewer**. Several **earthquake icons** (red circles) indicate where earthquakes were measured by the United States Geological Survey (USGS). Click on the largest circle to get specific information about the earthquake that occurred on January 12, 2010. Click on several other **earthquake icons** and ask students to discuss the location, magnitude, and date of the events relative to the January 12 event.

9 Have students write a news article or script for a newscast about the Haiti earthquake using what they observed in Google Earth (question 5).

Tracking the News *(cont.)*

Extension Activities

- **Fly to lat/long** 37 25 17 N 141 1 58 E. This is the site of the Fukushima Daiichi Power Plant that was struck by a large earthquake and tsunami on March 11, 2011. Have students use the **clock tool** and the **Earthquakes layer** to observe the effects of the disaster on the nuclear plant and write a news article.

- On August 4, 2010, 33 men were trapped underground for 69 days in a copper and gold mine called the San José Mine, located about 45 km (28 mi.) slightly northwest of Copiapó, Chile. Have students search for the site of the Copiapó mining accident and write a news report describing the difficulties involved in the rescue of the 33 men, based on the mine's location and its landscape.

Did You Know? ⊗

There are many magazines such as *National Geographic* that describe regions, cities, animals, and people around the world. The magazines provide a wealth of ideas for places to investigate using Google Earth.

User Tip

Be sure to turn off all layers in the **Layers panel** at the end of each lesson and do not save any layers in the **Temporary Places folder**. Having multiple layers on at the same time can slow down Google Earth.

Tracking the News *(cont.)*

Screenshot

Port-au-Prince, Haiti, January 2010

Name _____ Date _____

Earthquake Strikes!

1 Fly to for Port-au-Prince, Haiti, in Google Earth. Zoom in to the Presidential Palace (lat/long of 18 32 35 N 72 20 20 W and an Eye alt of about 450 m or 1,500 ft.), and use the clock tool to set the timeline slider to August 25, 2009. Describe what you see.

_____

_____

_____

2 Move the timeline slider ahead to January 16, 2010. Describe what you see.

_____

_____

_____

3 Move the timeline slider ahead to November 8, 2010. Describe what you see.

_____

_____

_____

4 Move the timeline slider backwards and forward and estimate how many months people lived in this "temporary housing."

_____

Earthquake Strikes! *(cont.)*

5 Write a news article or script for a news broadcast about the earthquake in Haiti using what you see in Google Earth.

_____

_____

_____

_____

_____

_____

_____

_____

_____

_____

_____

_____

_____

_____

_____

_____

Understanding the Water Cycle

Standards
Students understand the characteristics of ecosystems on Earth's surface. Students understand atmospheric processes and the water cycle.

Google Earth Tools

- Status bar: elev
- Status bar: Eye alt
- Toolbar: Ruler

Overview

Students will use Google Earth to explore the water cycle by following the path of water through the St. Lawrence drainage basin.

Vocabulary

- elevation
- locks
- runoff

Materials

- *Runoff Through the Great Lakes* activity sheets (pages 154–156)
- *Paddle-to-the-Sea* (Holling 1941) (optional)
- map of the Great Lakes in the United States (optional)

Procedure

1. Distribute copies of *Runoff Through the Great Lakes* activity sheets (pages 154–156) to students and review the water cycle. Have students complete question 1 on their activity sheets.

2. Read *Paddle-to-the-Sea* (Holling 1941) aloud to students.

3. Open Google Earth and navigate to a view of the northeast United States that includes all the Great Lakes and the St. Lawrence River (**Eye alt** of approximately 1,800 km or 1,100 mi.). Have students label the lakes on their maps and answer the questions on their activity sheets (questions 2 and 3).

4. Use the Great Lakes to demonstrate the runoff stage of the water cycle—how water from snowmelt flows downward to the ocean. Hover your cursor over each lake and observe the **elev** in the **Status bar**. Make your measurements close to the shore where the surface of the water appears as an image (see the *User Tip* on page 153). Have students write the **elev** of each lake on the map on their activity sheets (question 4). Have students draw arrows to show the direction of water flow from higher to lower elevations (question 4).

Understanding the Water Cycle *(cont.)*

Procedure *(cont.)*

5 Tell students that the elevation difference is greater between some lakes than others. **Fly to** Sault Ste. Marie, Michigan, located between Lake Superior and Lake Huron, at an **Eye alt** of about 50 km (30 mi.) and look for the Soo Locks in the river (46 30 13 N 84 21 3 W). Tell students that locks are devices used to move boats and ships up and down in elevation on a waterway that they would otherwise be unable to travel on. Gates allow water levels to be raised or lowered, creating a sort of escalator for ships. Have students write the **elev** of the river on the west (Lake Superior) and east (Lake Huron) sides of the locks on their activity sheets and calculate the difference (question 5).

6 **Fly to** Niagara Falls and **zoom** in to an **Eye alt** of about 2 km (8,000 ft.). Use the **zoom** and **Look joystick** to get a close-up perspective of Niagara Falls. Measure the elevation at the top and bottom of the falls. Ask students to write the difference in elevation from the top to the bottom of the falls on their activity sheets (question 5).

7 The Welland Canal was built to allow ships to travel between Lake Erie and Lake Ontario. A series of locks raises and lowers ships. Navigate along the Welland Canal and count the locks. (When the canal forks in two, stay with the eastern fork.) Have students record the number of locks on their activity sheets (question 7).

8 Follow the water through Lake Ontario, through the Thousand Islands, and into the Atlantic Ocean. Use the **ruler tool** (**Path tab** selected) to measure the distance that water travels from Lake Ontario to the Atlantic Ocean. Have students record this measurement on their activity sheets (question 8).

Extension Activity

Look at the Aral Sea in Kazakhstan and Uzbekistan; Lake Chad, Chad; the Dead Sea, Jordan/Israel/West Bank; and Mono Lake, California in Google Earth. Use the **clock tool** and the **timeline slider** to see if these lakes are changing over time. What impact will these changes have on the water cycle?

Understanding the Water Cycle *(cont.)*

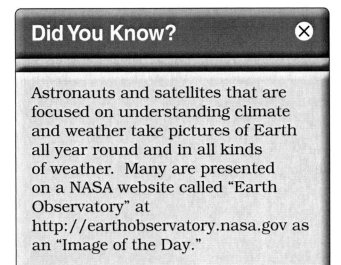

Did You Know? ✕

Astronauts and satellites that are focused on understanding climate and weather take pictures of Earth all year round and in all kinds of weather. Many are presented on a NASA website called "Earth Observatory" at http://earthobservatory.nasa.gov as an "Image of the Day."

User Tip

Elevation over the Great Lakes is a mixture of surface elevation and lake depth. Measure water-surface elevation near the shore.

Screenshot

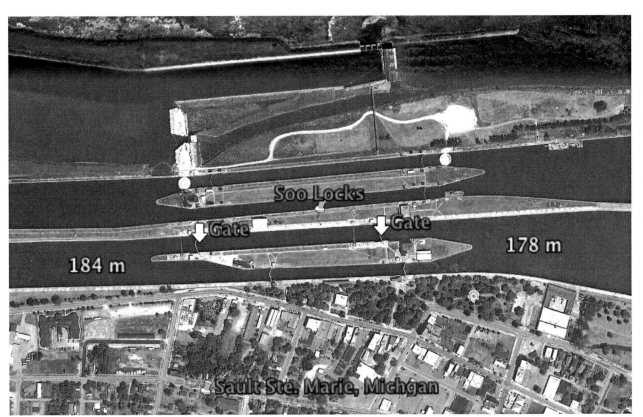

Soo Locks

Name _____ Date _____

Runoff Through the Great Lakes

 Write a brief description of each stage of the water cycle on the lines below.

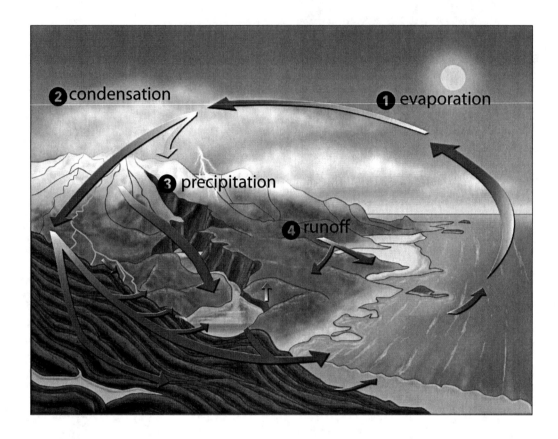

1. _____

2. _____

3. _____

4. _____

Runoff Through the Great Lakes *(cont.)*

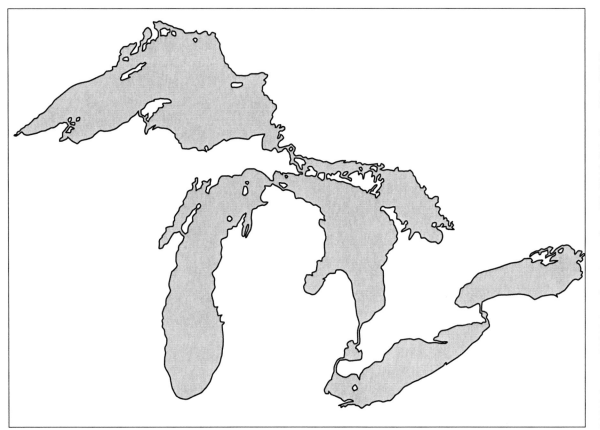

©2011 GOOGLE, ©2011 CNES/SPOT IMAGE, DATA SIO, NOAA, U.S. NAVY, NGA, GEBCO, IMAGE USDA FARM SERVICE AGENCY

2 Use Google Earth to help you label the lakes on the map above.

3 Are the Great Lakes connected? How do you know?

_____

_____

_____

4 Label the elevation of each lake on the map. Draw arrows to show the direction of water flow from lake to lake.

Runoff Through the Great Lakes *(cont.)*

5 Measure and record the elevation on each side of the Soo locks.

Elevation on west side of Soo locks: _____

Elevation on east side of Soo locks: _____

What is the difference in elevation between the west side of the locks towards Lake Superior and the east side towards Lake Huron?

_____

6 What is the difference in elevation from the top to the bottom of Niagara Falls?

_____

_____

7 How many locks do you see on the Welland Canal? _____

8 About how far does water travel from Ontario, Canada, to the Atlantic Ocean?

_____

_____

Discovering Forces of Change

Standards

Students know the physical processes that shape patterns on Earth's surface. Students know how features on Earth's surface are constantly changed by a combination of slow and rapid processes.

Google Earth Tools

- .kmz files
- Layers panel: Borders and Labels
- Layers panel: Gallery: Coastlines, Volcanoes*
- Places panel: Slider*
- Places panel: Temporary Places folder*
- Toolbar: Placemark, Ruler

Overview

Students will investigate changes on the surface of Earth caused by volcanoes, and will look in-depth at the results of the eruptions of Mt. Saint Helens and Mt. Vesuvius.

Vocabulary

- flank

Materials

- *Destructive Volcanoes* activity sheets (pages 161–162)
- books about volcanoes from the Recommended Literature list (Appendix F, pages 243–246)
- highlighters

Procedure

1. Ask students what they know about volcanoes. Read about how volcanoes change the surface of Earth in one of the books on the Recommended Literature list (Appendix F, pages 243–246), or show pictures of volcanoes. Distribute copies of the *Destructive Volcanoes* activity sheets (pages 161–162) to students and open Google Earth.

2. Turn off all folders and layers in the **Places panel** and **Layers panel.** Click on **Earth Gallery button** at the top of the **Layers panel.** This gallery displays **.kmz files** that have been submitted to Google Earth. Click on the **Nature tab** and then type "UNEP: Atlas of Our Changing Environment" into the **Search Earth Gallery box.** Click on **Open in Google Earth**, directly beneath the link. **Zoom** out until blue **UNEP icons** appear. These icons indicate places where change has occurred and can be seen using Google Earth images.

* Tool introduced in this lesson

Discovering Forces of Change *(cont.)*

Procedure *(cont.)*

3 In the **Temporary Places folder**, a new folder called **UNEP: Atlas of Our Changing Environment** will be automatically turned on. Open the folder by clicking the arrow down to see a list of **placemarks**.

4 Click once on the **Mount St. Helens placemark** to open a **UNEP window** featuring pictures and text from 1980, when Mount St. Helens erupted. Read the text aloud as students read it with you. Point out places in the images to which the text is referring. Ask students which image is more recent, the left or the right image. Have them write their answers on their activity sheets (question 1).

5 Click on **Overlay Images in Google Earth** in the **UNEP window**. Google Earth will **Fly to** Mount St. Helens and a transparent image will slowly load. A **Mount St. Helens, United States folder** will appear in the **Temporary Places folder**.

6 In the **Mount St. Helens, United States folder**, turn on all three boxes underneath that have dates (29 July 1972, 22 May 1983, and 07 September 1999). Beneath the **Mount St. Helens folder** in the **Places panel** is a **Places slider**. Slowly move the **Places slider** to the left, and then all the way to the right. (The date in the corner of the image will gradually change.) On their activity sheets, have students write three things that change in the image (question 2).

7 **Zoom** in and around the region. The first thing to occur during the 1980 eruption was the collapse of the north flank of the volcano. Show students the dome that has formed in the crater.

8 Turn off the **Mount St. Helens folder** in the **Temporary Places folder**. Use the **navigation tools** to navigate to a current view that highlights the collapsed north flank and the dome. Use the **ruler tool** to measure the crater and have students write the distance on their activity sheets (question 3).

Discovering Forces of Change *(cont.)*

Procedure *(cont.)*

9 In the **Layers panel**, open **Gallery** and turn on **Volcanoes**. Turn on the **Borders and Labels layer** as well and **zoom** out so Washington and Oregon appear in the **3D viewer**. Ask students if Washington or Oregon has more volcanoes, and have them write their answers on their activity sheets (question 4). Mount St. Helens is one of the Cascade volcanoes that run along the northwest coast of the United States through northern California, Oregon, and Washington.

10 Look for Mt. Rainier in Washington. It is one of the largest and most classic appearing of the Cascade volcanoes. **Zoom** in to have students investigate this volcano, and have students answer question 5 on their activity sheets.

Did You Know?

A lava dome is a circular mound formed by the slow flow of lava from a volcano. Lava domes evolve over time and can eventually collapse, solidify, or erode. Lava domes often grow in the crater of a volcano, but can also form independently as with Lassen Peak, California, one of the largest lava domes in the world.

User Tip

Many of the **Earth Gallery layers** are also in the **Global Awareness layer** in the **Layers panel**.

Extension Activities

- Open Google Earth and **Fly to** Mt. Vesuvius, Italy, and **zoom** to an **Eye alt** of 9 km (30,000 ft.). Look for the volcano's crater and evidence of past eruptions in the form of ridges radiating from the center of the volcano.

- **Fly to** Pompeii, Italy, and look for the evacuated ruins, just west of the city center (lat/long 40 45 04 N 14 29 42 E). Pompeii was buried under 15 feet of ash but has since been excavated. Have students write a report about Mt. Vesuvius, emphasizing what they observe in google Earth.

Discovering Forces of Change *(cont.)*

Screenshots

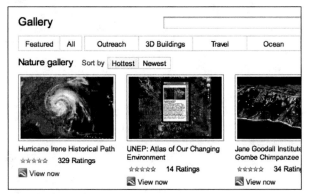

Earth Gallery

Mount St. Helens

Name _____ Date _____

Destructive Volcanoes

 Look at the two images below. Put a check mark by the image you think is more recent.

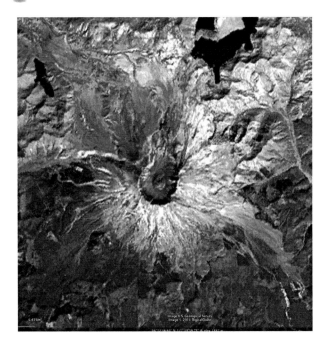 

 In Google Earth, slowly move the Places slider beneath the Mount St. Helens folder all the way to the left and then to the right. Write three differences you notice between the pictures.

_____

_____

_____

_____

_____

_____

Destructive Volcanoes *(cont.)*

3 Use the ruler tool to measure the crater on the north flank of the volcano. What is the measurement?

_____

4 Does Oregon or Washington have more volcanoes?

_____

5 Investigate Mount Rainier in Washington. Do you think this volcano has erupted recently? Why or why not?

_____

_____

_____

_____

_____

Shading the Earth

Standards
Students know how Earth's position relative to the Sun affects events and conditions on Earth. Students know that the Sun provides the light and heat necessary to maintain the temperature of Earth.

Google Earth Tools

- Toolbar: Sun*

Overview

Students will study the Sun and the shadow patterns it makes on our planet.

Vocabulary

- revolve
- rotate

Materials

- *Night and Day* activity sheets (pages 166–168)
- colored pencils
- highlighters

Procedure

1 Distribute colored pencils and copies of the *Night and Day* activity sheets (pages 166–168) to students and open Google Earth.

2 **Zoom** out to a full view of Earth with north facing up. Show students that Earth always appears in daylight in the **3D viewer**. Ask students to refer to the diagram of Earth on their activity sheets (question 1). Based on the location of the sun, ask students to color half the Earth in shadow (question 1). Ask students how they decided where to draw their shadows.

3 Click on the **sun tool** in the **Toolbar**. A **sun slider** will appear in the upper left corner of the **3D viewer**. Move the **sun slider** backwards and forwards. Ask students to follow the shadows on Earth. Have them draw an arrow on the diagram on their activity sheets indicating which direction the shadows travel (question 2).

* Tool introduced in this lesson

Shading the Earth *(cont.)*

Procedure *(cont.)*

4 Click once on the button that looks like a magnifying glass with a (–) on it in the **sun slider panel**. Ask students to notice the time span that is being measured (*one day, one week, one month, one year*). Continue to click the (–) and have students answer question 3 on their activity sheets.

5 In Google Earth, it appears as though the sun revolves around Earth, when in reality, Earth revolves around the sun in a year and rotates around its own axis in a day. Ask two students to stand and demonstrate this by asking one student to portray the sun and one student to portray Earth.

6 Click the (+) or (–) magnifying glasses until the time span represents one day. Click on the **play button** in the **sun slider panel** (it looks like a clock with an arrow on it) and watch Earth rotate through one day.

7 Navigate to a view of Earth with the North Pole in the center of the **3D viewer**. Click the **play button** and observe the movement of the shadow on Earth. Repeat this step for the South Pole and have students answer question 4 on their activity sheets.

8 Navigate back to the North Pole. Click on the **sun slider** and move the **sun slider** so the time extent is one year. Move slowly through the month of January and the month of June. On their activity sheets, have students describe what it would be like to live at the North Pole for a day in January and a day in June (question 5).

Extension Activities

- When the sun is above a place on Earth during the day, shadows are made behind everything that is tall. Have students investigate the buildings listed below and write the compass direction that the shadow is cast (N, S, E, or W).

  ➤ Queensland Number One, Gold Coast, Australia

  ➤ Eiffel Tower, Paris, France

  ➤ London Eye, London, England

- **Zoom** out to a global view of Earth. In the **Layers panel**, open the **Gallery layer**, then **NASA,** and then **Earth City Lights**. Turn on the **Earth City Lights layer** to see the entire Earth as if it were nighttime. What do the lights reveal about population distribution?

Shading the Earth *(cont.)*

Screenshots

sun tool

play button

sun slider panel

South Pole in Spring

DATA SIO, NOAA, U.S. NAVY, NGA, GEBCO

Name _____ Date _____

Night and Day

 1 Color half of the Earth in shadow. Use the location of the sun to help you decide which half of Earth to color.

 2 As you move the sun slider in Google Earth, draw an arrow on the diagram above to indicate which direction the shadows travel.

Night and Day *(cont.)*

3 As you click on the (–) in the sun slider panel, write down the increments of time that are represented.

_____   _____

_____   _____

4 Navigate to a view of Earth with the North Pole in the center of the 3D viewer. Click on the play button in the sun slider panel and watch the shadows of the sun. Then, navigate to a view of Earth with the South Pole in the center of the 3D viewer. Click on the play button and watch the shadow move. Is there a place on Earth that stays light (with the sun shining on it) the whole day through? If yes, where is it? Why do you think this is?

_____

_____

_____

_____

_____

Night and Day *(cont.)*

5 Adjust the sun slider settings so the full time extent is one year. Use the cursor to move slowly through a month in January and again in June. On the lines below, describe what it would be like to live at the North Pole for a day in January and a day in June.

_____

_____

_____

_____

_____

_____

_____

_____

_____

_____

_____

Using Energy

Standards

Standards
Students know the relationships between economic activities and resources. Students know the sources and properties of energy.

Google Earth Tools
- Layers panel: Global Awareness: Appalachian Mountaintop Removal*
- Layers panel: Borders and Labels, Roads
- Places panel: Temporary Places folder
- Toolbar: Placemark

Overview
Students will discover how the Sun is ultimately responsible for most of our energy sources, and will explore these sources of energy, including renewable and nonrenewable.

Vocabulary
- fossil fuels
- geothermal
- nonrenewable
- renewable
- solar

Materials
- *Fuel Sources* activity sheets (pages 173–174)
- colored pencils or markers

Tool introduced in this lesson

Procedure

1 Discuss with students the sources of energy that help us run our lives. Explain that coal and oil come from giant swamp forests and tiny sea creatures called diatoms that existed during the time of the dinosaurs. They were buried over time and decomposed until they became coal and oil. Now they are being dug up and used to power our homes, cars, and toys. That is why we call coal and oil "fossil fuels."

2 Distribute copies of the *Fuel Sources* activity sheets (pages 173–174) to students and open Google Earth.

3 Many kinds of mining operations are visible in Google Earth. Turn on the **Borders and Labels layer.** Open the **Global Awareness layer** and turn on the **Appalachian Mountaintop Removal layer**. Double-click on the layer itself. Point out to students the **Appalachian Mountaintop Removal icons** indicating the location of mountaintop mines. On their activity sheets, have students write down which states have mountaintop removal coal mines (question 1).

Using Energy *(cont.)*

Procedure *(cont.)*

4 Navigate to the mines in Kentucky and move the cursor over the **Appalachian Mountaintop Removal icons** until you find the Montgomery Creek Mine at Montgomery Creek, Kentucky (it is toward the south end of the group). **Zoom** in until the yellow box fills the **3D viewer**. Click on the **Historic Image Overlay icon** in the upper left corner of the yellow box to see before and after pictures of the Montgomery Creek area in pop-up window.

5 Click on the left image to see the area before mountaintop removal. Look in the **Temporary Places folder** for this overlay and click it on and off, or use the slider below the **Places panel** to see it change gradually. On their activity sheets, have students write down some of the impacts mountaintop removal might have on the local environment in the mountains of Kentucky (question 2). **Placemark** the Montgomery Creek mine and save it in your *Science* folder.

6 **Fly to** the coal mines listed on students' activity sheets, **placemark** them and observe them. Have students answer question 3.

7 **Fly to** to Drax, England, and **zoom** in on the coal-fired power plant (northwest of town). Explain to students that when coal is burned, it produces heat, water vapor, and carbon dioxide. The heat is used to make electricity. The white billowing clouds are the water vapor. The colorless carbon dioxide goes into the atmosphere and becomes a greenhouse gas. Ask students to identify piles of coal and clouds of vapor.

8 Tell students that coal and oil are nonrenewable sources of energy, which means that once they have been used, they are gone forever. There are renewable alternatives. We can use the energy of the sun through solar panels that catch the sun's energy and convert it to electricity. **Fly to** Google Headquarters, Mountain View, California, to see solar panels on the roofs of buildings. Have students sketch a solar panel in the first box in question 3.

9 Explain to students that another source of renewable energy is wind. Wind farms can be seen in deserts and in the ocean. **Fly to** Altamont Pass, California, turn on the **Roads layer,** and look to the north and south of Highway 580 for large wind turbines. Have students sketch and color a wind turbine in the second box labeled *wind* in question 4 on their activity sheets.

Using Energy *(cont.)*

Procedure *(cont.)*

 10 Tell students that geothermal energy captures heat from under the surface of the Earth to create electricity. **Fly to** Mammoth Lakes, California. Look about 3 miles east of town for the Mammoth Pacific geothermal plant (37 38 45 N 118 54 34 W). Have students sketch the plant in the box labeled *geothermal* in question 4.

Extension Activities

- **Placemark** these oil fields: Al Uthmaniya to Haradh, Saudi Arabia (24 49 14 N 49 14 11 E); Denver City, Texas (32 57 52 N 102 49 45 W); Prudhoe Bay, Alaska (70 14 12 N 148 30 07 W). Have students find common characteristics of oil fields.

- Look for other places on Earth where energy is generated. Consider geothermal, nuclear, and hydropower options. Have students compare the advantages and disadvantages for each type of energy.

Did You Know?

A group of solar panels covering a large area out in the open is called a *solar farm*. Some solar farms use solar panels that capture the sun's energy directly and convert it into electricity. A circular solar farm is made up of mirrors that reflect the sunlight onto a central tower containing water that is heated and used to make electricity. You can see both kinds three miles east of Dagget, California. **Zoom** in to distinguish the solar farms from agricultural fields.

Using Energy *(cont.)*

Screenshots

© GOOGLE

Appalachian Mountaintop
Removal layer

© 2011 DIGITAL GLOBE IMAGE USDA FARM SERVICE
AGENCY. © 2011 GOOGLE

Montgomery Creek, KY Appalachian
Mountaintop Removal window

IMAGE USDA FARM SERVICE AGENCY, IMAGE ©2011 COMMONWEALTH OF
VIRGINIA, IMAGE ©2011 DIGITALGLOBE

Windmills, Altamont Pass, California

Name _____ Date _____

Fuel Sources

1 List the states that have mountaintop removal coal mines.

_____

_____

2 In Google Earth, look at the area around the Montgomery Creek Mine before and after mountaintop removal. What are some ways that mountaintop removal has impacted the local environment in the mountains of Kentucky?

_____

_____

3 Fly to the following coal mines and add a placemark for each one in Google Earth.

- Gongwusuzhen, Inner Mongolia, China region

  39 20 N 106 55 E

- Gevra, India (southeast of the city)

  22 20 N 82 36 E

- Antelope Coalmine Road, Douglas, Wyoming

  43 28 N 105 20 W

On the lines below, list three common characteristics of coal mines.

_____

_____

_____

Fuel Sources *(cont.)*

 In the boxes below, draw and color some different ways we get energy from the sun, the wind, and Earth.

Solar

Wind

Geothermal

Building a Capital

Google Earth Tools

- Status bar: Eye alt
- Toolbar: Placemark
- Toolbar: Ruler: Heading*

Overview

Students will apply their math skills and use Google Earth to explore the city plan for Washington, DC.

Vocabulary

- capital
- Capitol
- heading

Materials

- *Washington, DC* activity sheets (pages 178–180)

Procedure

1 Introduce students to the famous landmarks and monuments of Washington, DC. Discuss the concept of a capital city. Distribute copies of the *Washington, DC* activity sheets (pages 178–180) to students, and have them write the definition of a *capital* (question 1). Open Google Earth.

2 In 1791, the United States built a new capital along the Potomac River. **Fly to** Washington, DC, and **placemark** it in your *History* folder. Ask students if they can identify any of the features in and around the capital. On their activity sheets, ask students to write the features they can identify in Washington, DC. (question 2).

3 Look at the street patterns in Washington, DC from an **Eye alt** of about 4.5 km (16,000 ft.). Ask students to write down on their activity sheets some geometric patterns they observe in the city (question 3). If using an interactive whiteboard, have students use the pen tool to trace some of the shapes and patterns.

* Tool introduced in this lesson

Building a Capital *(cont.)*

Procedure *(cont.)*

4 In addition to length, the **ruler tool** also measures **heading** (an angular direction relative to north). Open the **ruler tool** and click once on top of the White House. Move the cursor around and call students' attention to how the **heading** changes.

5 Move the cursor down Pennsylvania Avenue and click to mark a second point on top of the Capitol. Ask students to write down the **heading** on their activity sheets and look at the measurement to determine how many miles separate the two buildings (question 4). Click **Save** in the **Ruler window** to save this line so it will appear in the **3D viewer**.

6 **Fly to** and **placemark** the places listed on students' activity sheets and have students measure their headings relative to the White House, as well as their distance from the White House (question 5). Save each ruler line so they appear in the **3D viewer**. Ask students if they can determine a pattern in these lines.

7 Use the **ruler tool** to measure from the Capitol building to the Jefferson Memorial and from the Jefferson Memorial to the White House. Have students write these measurements on their activity sheets (question 6) and save these lines so they appear in the **3D viewer**. Ask students if they see a pattern in these lines.

8 Find and **placemark** the Lincoln Memorial (at the west end of the Washington Mall). Ask students why they think this monument deviates from the pattern (question 7).

Did You Know?

Pierre Charles L'Enfant was commissioned by George Washington to design Washington, DC. He was a fan of math and used his math skills to make a very creative city with avenues radiating out from rectangles.

Building a Capital *(cont.)*

Extension Activity

Have students look for a star formed by the diagonal roads north of the White House. Hint: The star is upside down with the White House at the bottom. Students can use the **path tool** to outline the star.

Screenshot

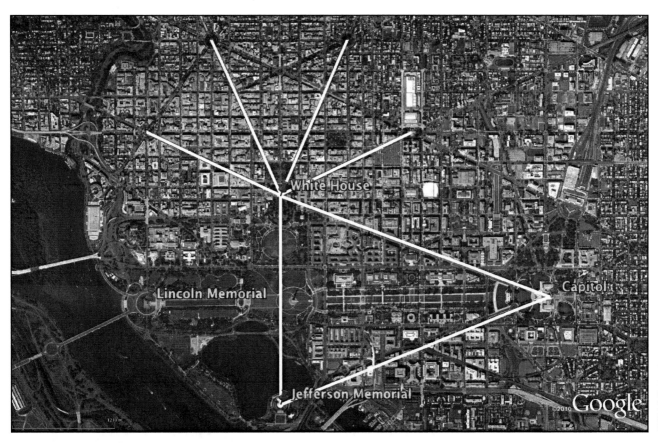

Washington, DC

Name _____ Date _____

Washington, DC

1 On the lines below, write a definition for *capital*.

_____

_____

2 Fly to Washington, DC in Google Earth. What are some features you can identify?

_____

_____

_____

_____

3 Draw and label the geometric shapes or patterns you observe.

Washington, DC *(cont.)*

4   Open the ruler tool and click once on top of the White House. Move the cursor down Pennsylvania Avenue and click a second point on top of the Capitol. Write down the heading.

_____

Read the measurement. How many miles separate the two buildings?

_____

5   Find the following places in Google Earth. Next to each place, write the heading (from the White House) and the distance in miles.

DuPont Circle

     Heading: _____

     Distance: _____

Washington Circle

     Heading: _____

     Distance: _____

Logan Circle

     Heading: _____

     Distance: _____

Mt. Vernon Square

     Heading: _____

     Distance: _____

Washington, DC *(cont.)*

6 Measure the distance between the following landmarks.

Capitol building to Jefferson Memorial: _____

Jefferson Memorial to White House: _____

7 Based on the pattern of lines you see, where should the Lincoln Memorial be sited to fit the pattern?

_____

Why do you think it was built in its current position?

_____

Estimating Deforestation

Standards

Students know ways in which humans can change ecosystems. Students use specific strategies to estimate quantities and measurements (e.g., estimating the whole by estimating the parts).

Google Earth Tools

- Status bar: Eye alt
- Toolbar: Clock, Ruler
- Toolbar: Polygon*

Overview

Students will estimate deforestation in the Amazon.

Vocabulary

- deforestation

Materials

- *Subtracting the Amazon* activity sheets (pages 184–186)
- *The Lorax* (Seuss 1971) or another book about saving forests (*optional*)

Procedure

1 Read aloud to students a section of *The Lorax* (Seuss 1971) or another book about saving forests. Discuss with students what happened to the truffula trees and how they might have been saved.

2 Distribute copies of the *Subtracting the Amazon* activity sheets (pages 184–186) to students and open Google Earth. **Fly to** Rondonia, Brazil, at an **Eye alt** of 480 km (300 mi.). **Placemark** Rondonia and add it to your *Science* folder. Use the **navigation tools** to investigate the area and ask students to describe what they see on their activity sheets (question 1).

3 **Fly to** 10 03 S 64 08 W at an **Eye alt** of 300 km (200 mi.) and look for a dark rectangle. **Zoom** until the rectangle fills the **3D viewer** (**Eye alt** of 30 km or 20 mi.). This is a recent image. Open the **timeline slider** by clicking on the **clock tool** in the **Toolbar**. Use the **timeline slider** to travel back in time to see how the forest changed from June 1975 to October 2009. Ask students to summarize what they observe on their activity sheets (question 2).

* Tool introduced in this lesson

Estimating Deforestation *(cont.)*

Procedure *(cont.)*

4 Close the **timeline slider** to return to the current view of Rondonia. Tell students that the dark rectangle will define a sample area. They will measure cleared fields within this sample area to determine the amount of deforestation. Have students use the **ruler tool** to measure the width and height of the sample area in miles to determine its area. Have them record this information on their activity sheets (question 3).

5 Within the sample area, choose a roughly rectangular cleared field to measure. Click on the **polygon tool** in the **Toolbar** and name the **polygon** *Area 1.* Move the cursor (which will be a square) to the first corner of the cleared field and hold down the mouse. Click on the next corner and proceed around the area until all four corners are clicked. Remind students that you are estimating areas, not trying to get exact measurements. Click **OK** to close the **Polygon window**.

6 Use the **ruler tool** to measure the width and height of the rectangle. Have students record the measurements and calculate the area of the rectangle in the box labeled *Area 1* on their activity sheets (question 4).

7 Continue to measure additional cleared areas and label them *Area 2* through *Area 6*, until all the areas are measured and recorded on students' activity sheets (question 4). Again, emphasize to students that they are estimating areas, not trying to be exact. Have students add all six areas together and write the sum (question 5).

8 When all the areas have been measured, have students add them up and divide the sum of the areas of the cleared fields by the area of the sample (the dark rectangle). Then have students multiply by 100 to get the percent of cleared forest in this rectangle (question 6).

9 Navigate around the Amazon forest. Can the estimate you determined for one region represent the whole Amazon forest? Ask students to write what they think on their activity sheets (question 7).

Extension Activity

Ask students to estimate the percent of deforestation per year by dividing the percent by the number of years since the forest was untouched.

(*Hint*: Use the **clock tool**.)

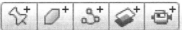

Estimating Deforestation *(cont.)*

Did You Know?

Benjamin Franklin said, "By clearing America of woods Americans were scouring our Planet—and so making this Side of our Globe reflect a brighter Light to the Eyes of the Inhabitants of Mars or Venus."

Screenshot

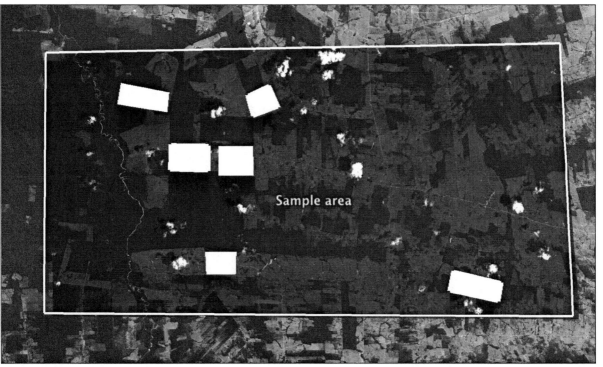

Rectangle northwest of
Rondonia

Name _____ Date _____

Subtracting the Amazon

1 Fly to Rondonia, Brazil, at an Eye alt of 480 km (300 mi.). Describe what you see.

_____

_____

_____

_____

2 Use the clock tool and the timeline slider to travel back in time to see how the forest changed from June 1975 to October 2009. Summarize what you observed on the lines below.

_____

_____

_____

_____

_____

3 Write the measurements of the sample area (dark rectangle) and calculate the area.

length: _____

width: _____

area of rectangle: _____

Subtracting the Amazon *(cont.)*

4 Write the appropriate measurements and calculate the areas of the rectangular fields.

Area 1:

length: _____

width: _____

area of rectangle: _____

Area 4:

length: _____

width: _____

area of rectangle: _____

Area 2:

length: _____

width: _____

area of rectangle: _____

Area 5:

length: _____

width: _____

area of rectangle: _____

Area 3:

length: _____

width: _____

area of rectangle: _____

Area 6:

length: _____

width: _____

area of rectangle: _____

5 Sum of areas of 6 cleared fields = _____

Subtracting the Amazon *(cont.)*

6 Use the following steps to find the approximate percentage of forest that has been cleared:

_____ ÷ _____ = _____ x 100 = _____ % cleared

Sum of areas of 6   Area of sample
cleared fields

7 Can the estimate you determined for one region represent the whole Amazon forest? Why or why not?

_____

_____

_____

_____

_____

_____

Measuring America

Google Earth Tools

- Layers panel: More: Transporation: Rail*
- Layers panel: Roads
- Status bar: Eye alt
- Toolbar: Polygon, Ruler

Overview

By observing the results of The Ordinance of 1785 in South Dakota, students will use their math skills to appreciate the relevance of a 40-acre plot of land.

Vocabulary

- section
- surveyor

Materials

- *Plots of Land* activity sheets (pages 190–192)

Procedure

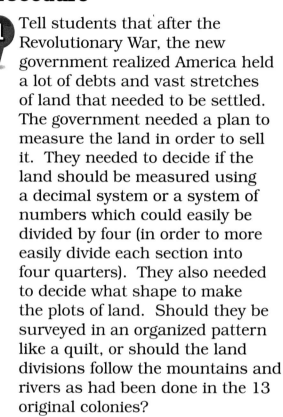

1. Tell students that after the Revolutionary War, the new government realized America held a lot of debts and vast stretches of land that needed to be settled. The government needed a plan to measure the land in order to sell it. They needed to decide if the land should be measured using a decimal system or a system of numbers which could easily be divided by four (in order to more easily divide each section into four quarters). They also needed to decide what shape to make the plots of land. Should they be surveyed in an organized pattern like a quilt, or should the land divisions follow the mountains and rivers as had been done in the 13 original colonies?

2. Distribute copies of the *Plots of Land* activity sheets (pages 190–192) and open Google Earth.

3. **Fly to** Lynchburg, South Carolina at an altitude of about 9 km (30,000 ft.). Look at the patterns of the fields. This land was settled before the Revolutionary War. Show students how there is no organized pattern to the fields. Ask them to determine any geometric shapes they see and to write their answers on their activity sheets (question 1).

* Tool introduced in this lesson

Measuring America *(cont.)*

Procedure *(cont.)*

4 **Fly to** Mt. Vernon, South Dakota, at the same **Eye alt** at which you viewed Lynchburg. This land was surveyed after the Revolutionary War. Ask students to identify some of the geometric shapes they observe in Google Earth and write their answers on their activity sheets (question 2). Have students compare what they have seen to answer question 3.

5 **Zoom** to an **Eye alt** of about 64,000 km (40,000 ft.) and call students' attention to how the land is divided. Point out a square section, and tell students this piece of land is oriented with its sides running north and south, and east and west. Use the **ruler tool** to determine the size of each section (question 4).

6 Have students use the information on their activity sheets to determine the number of acres in a quarter-quarter section (question 5).

7 Sections were organized into townships that were approximately square with six sections on a side. Have students calculate how many square miles are in each township, using the information on their activity sheets (question 6).

8 Explain that within a township, sections were numbered starting with the northeast section as number 1. Have students number the sections on their activity sheets (question 7).

9 Find the town of Mt. Vernon in Google Earth. If it was in section 22, which was section 1? Use the **polygon tool** to draw a square around that section in Google Earth. Turn on the **Roads layer** and have students write the two streets that border section 1 on their activity sheets (question 8).

10 Tell students that a horse and wagon could travel about 10 or 12 miles in a day. Ask students to answer questions 9 and 10 on their activity sheets.

11 In the **Layers panel**, open the **More layer**, then **Transportation**, and then turn on the **Rail layer**. Look for the black line that connects Mt. Vernon to Betts and Mitchell to the east. Tell students that a steam train traveled about 35 miles per hour. Have students answer question 11 on their activity sheets.

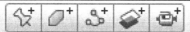

Measuring America *(cont.)*

Extension Activity

Fly to the agricultural regions listed below at an **Eye alt** of 16 km (10 mi.) and describe each region using geometric terms and patterns. What was probably the dominant geographic factor in determining the shapes of these fields?

- Ainsworth, Nebraska
- North Lancaster, Canada
- Yoder, Wyoming
- Traver, California

Did You Know?

Geometry (*geo* = land; *metr* = measure) took root in the valleys of the Tigris and the Nile as civilizations developed agriculture along the floodplains. Fields had to be reestablished each year after the annual floods, and geometry allowed the farmers to make these measurements efficiently. The skill of these early surveyors is apparent in the nearly perfect north-south orientation of the Great Pyramid of Giza.

Screenshot

Mt. Vermont, South Dakota

Name _____ Date _____

Plots of Land

1 Look at Lynchburg, South Carolina, in Google Earth at an Eye alt of about 9 km (30,000 ft.). Look at the patterns of the fields. What geometric shapes do you see?

_____

_____

_____

2 Look at Mt. Vernon, South Dakota, in Google Earth at an Eye alt of about 9 km (30,000 ft.). Look at the patterns of the fields. What geometric shapes do you see?

_____

_____

_____

3 What was different about the way land was divided after the war?

_____

_____

_____

4 Use the ruler tool to determine the uniform size of each section of land.

length: _____

width: _____

Plots of Land *(cont.)*

 5 There are 640 acres in a section. If a section is divided into quarters, it is called a quarter section, and if it is again divided into quarters, it is called a quarter-quarter section. How many acres are in a quarter-quarter section?

_____

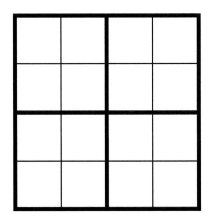

 6 Sections were organized into townships that consisted of six sections per side. How many square miles were in each township?

_____

 7 Within a township, sections were numbered starting with the northeast section as number 1. In the chart below, assign a number to the remaining sections, first moving west to the end of the row, then south one row, then east to the end of the row, then south one row, and so on.

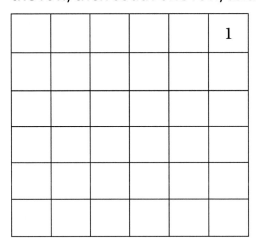

Plots of Land *(cont.)*

8 Find the town of Mt. Vernon in Google Earth. If it was in section 22, which section was 1? Draw a polygon around that section in Google Earth and turn on the Roads layer. Record the two streets that border section 1.

_____

Zoom out and navigate east to the town of Mitchell. Without using the ruler tool, determine the distance between Mt. Vernon and Mitchell.

_____

10 A horse and wagon could travel about 10 or 12 miles in a day. How many miles per hour is that?

_____

How long would it take for a farmer to travel from Mt. Vernon to Mitchell with his horse and wagon?

_____

A steam train could travel about 35 miles per hour. How long would it take to travel by steam train from Mt. Vernon to Mitchell?

_____

Designing Crops

Standards
Students know how human activities have increased the ability of the physical environment to support human life in the local community, state, United States, and other countries. Students understand the basic measures of perimeter, area, volume, capacity, mass, angle, and circumference.

Google Earth Tools

- Places panel: Places slider
- Status bar: Eye alt
- Toolbar: Image Overlay*
- Toolbar: Ruler

Overview

Students will continue to explore Google Earth and use their math skills to understand crop geometries.

Vocabulary

- pivot
- radius

Materials

- *Water All Around* activity sheets (pages 196–198)
- straws
- string
- tape or stapler

Procedure

1 Ask students what shape a crop field should be and why. Are all fields square? Why would a field be rectangular? Can students imagine a circular field? Why would a farmer want a circular field?

2 Distribute copies of the *Water All Around* activity sheets (pages 196–198) to students and open Google Earth.

3 Navigate around the Haxtun area at an **Eye alt** of about 15 km (50,000 ft.). Ask students to write down the names of the shapes of the fields on their activity sheets (question 1). Have them think of a reason why some of these fields are circles and write their answers on their activity sheets (question 2).

4 Explain that these crops are irrigated using a center pivot irrigation system. Point out the photograph on their activity sheets and have them read about how the pivot system works (question 3).

* Tool introduced in this lesson

Designing Crops *(cont.)*

Procedure *(cont.)*

5 Distribute one straw and a piece of string to each student. Ask students to push the string into the straw so that about 2.5 cm (1 in.) of string is inside the straw, and several inches are outside the straw. Have students secure the string in the straw using tape or staples.

6 Have students hold the straw vertically (string end down) in the center of the circle on their activity sheets (question 3), and hold the string so that it reaches one edge of the circle. Tell students this is called the *radius* of the circle. Ask students to use this model to help them write an explanation of how the pivot irrigation system works (question 4).

7 Choose a circular field north of Haxtun. To find the area of the circular field, use the **ruler tool** to measure the radius of the field in yards. Ask students to write this radius on their activity sheets (question 5) and calculate the area of the field in square yards using the formula for area: πr^2, where π is 3.14 (question 6).

8 Have students calculate the area of the square field around the circular one they just measured and answer question 7 on their activity sheets.

9 The water for these center pivot fields comes from the Ogallala Aquifer. To find where this aquifer is, open your web browser and go to http://en.wikipedia.org/wiki/Ogallala _Aquifer. Right-click on the first map of the aquifer and select **Save as**. **Save** the image to your desktop.

10 Return to Google Earth and navigate to a view of the lower 48 United States. Click on the **Image Overlay tool** in the **Toolbar**. Select **Browse** and select the map you just saved. Click **Open** and the map will appear in Google Earth. Drag the green corners of the map to move them around until the map approximately matches the state borders in Google Earth. Click **OK** to close the **Image Overlay window**. Use the **Places slider** under the **Places panel** to make the map transparent. Investigate the shape of the fields over the aquifer.

Designing Crops *(cont.)*

Extension Activities

- Compare the circular fields in Saudi Arabia (about 80 km or 50 mi. west of Riyadh) to those in Colorado. How are they similar, and how are they different?
- Have students search Saudi Arabia for evidence of fields that no longer produce crops (e.g., at 27 27 49 N 47 34 57 E). Ask students to research what happened to the water.

Did You Know?

An aquifer is a large but shallow underground water source. The Ogallala Aquifer, also known as the High Plains Aquifer, is located beneath the Great Plains in the United States, including parts of Colorado. Center pivot irrigation is common above the aquifer since it is easy to sink a well and set up a sprinkler above it.

Screenshot

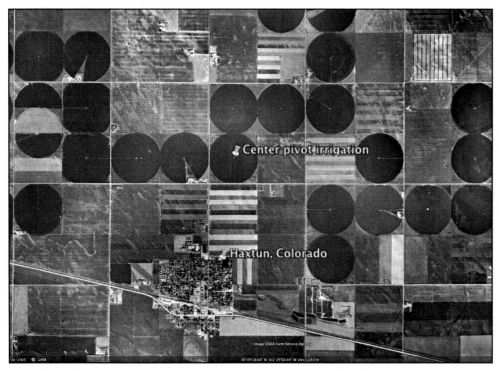

Haxtun, Colorado: center pivot irrigation fields

Name _____ Date _____

Water All Around

1 Describe the shapes of the fields around Haxtun, Colorado.

_____

_____

2 Why do you think some of the fields are circles?

_____

_____

_____

_____

Directions: Look at the photo and read the description below of center pivot irrigation. Then, complete the activity and answer the questions on the following pages.

In a pivot irrigation system, an underground well supplies water to the center of the field. The water comes up through a pipe and runs through a long sprinkler system that moves around the field in a circle.

Water All Around *(cont.)*

 3 Your teacher will give you a straw and some string. Follow the directions below to create a model of a pivot irrigation system.

- Push the string into the straw so that about 2.5 cm (1 in.) of string is inside the straw, and several inches are outside the straw.

- Secure the string in the straw using tape or staples.

- Hold the straw vertically in the center of the circle below with the string end touching the paper.

- Hold the string so that it touches the outside edge of the circle and rotate the string around the circle.

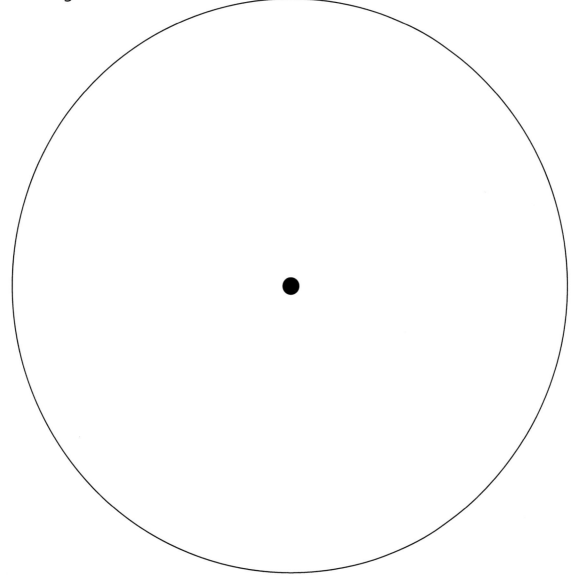

Water All Around *(cont.)*

 On the lines below, explain how the pivot irrigation system works.

_____

_____

_____

5 Use the ruler tool to measure the radius of a circular field in yards.

radius = _____ yd.

 Calculate the area of the field in square yards using the formula for area:

πr^2 (where π is 3.14)

area = _____ yd².

7 Measure the side of the square field in which the circular field sits. Calculate the area of the field in square yards.

sides = _____ yd.

area = _____ yd².

Exploring Space

Standards

Students know that astronomical objects in space are massive in size and are separated from one another by vast distances. Students understand the impact of postwar scientific research on contemporary society (e.g., the U.S. space program).

Google Earth Tools

- Layers panel: Moon Gallery: Apollo Missions*
- Places panel: My Places folder
- Status bar: Eye alt
- Toolbar: Placemark, Ruler
- Toolbar: Planets*

Overview

Students will use all their Google Earth skills as they travel to the Moon to explore the Apollo landing sites as well as the craters and lava seas that make the Moon different shades of gray.

Vocabulary

- asteroids
- crater
- erode
- mare
- mission

Materials

- *To the Moon* activity sheets (pages 203–204)
- *Full Moon* (Light 1999) (optional)
- *Moonshot: The Flight of Apollo 11* (Floca 2009) (optional)

Procedure

1 Read *Moonshot: The Flight of Apollo 11* (Floca 2009), or another book about the Moon or the Apollo missions, or show students some photographs from *Full Moon* (Light 1999).

2 Tell students that besides exploring Earth, they can use Google Earth to explore the Moon, Mars, and the sky using the **planets tool**. Distribute copies of the *To the Moon* activity sheets (pages 203–204) to students and open Google Earth.

3 Turn off all folders in your **My Places folder**, as well as any layers in the **Layers panel**. Click on the **planets tool** in the **Toolbar** and choose **Moon**.

4 **Zoom** out and rotate the Moon. Ask students to describe what they see on their activity sheets (question 1). Point out the darker areas which are large regions of ancient lava. These are called *mare*, which means sea, because they were once thought to be seas.

* Tool introduced in this lesson

Exploring Space *(cont.)*

Procedure *(cont.)*

5 Rotate the Moon to the brighter side that is covered with craters. **Fly to** Gamow and **placemark** it. The crater should fill the **3D viewer** at an **Eye alt** of about 200 km (130 mi.). Use the **ruler tool** to measure the diameter of Gamow Crater and have students write the diameter on their activity sheets (question 2). Point out how some craters seem to overlap each other. Explain that this means that the overlapping craters are younger because the meteor impact that created the crater happened more recently than the craters underneath. Ask students to decide if smaller craters on top of Gamow are younger or older than Gamow.

6 Tell students that the Moon was bombarded with meteors and asteroids about 3.9 billion years ago. So was Earth. But on Earth, the craters have eroded due to their exposure to wind and water. There is no wind or water on the Moon, so the craters remain. Tell students we could still find the footprints of the astronauts who landed there if another mission flew to the Moon.

7 Direct students' attention to the **Layers panel**. Does it look different from how it looks when students are viewing Earth? Open the **Moon Gallery layer**, and then open and turn on the **Apollo Missions layer** to see a view of the Moon that shows all six landing sites (marked by icons of astronauts holding flags). Have students solve the math problem in question 3.

8 Double-click on the **Apollo 12 layer** in the **Layers panel** to see the landing site. **Zoom** in to an **Eye alt** of about 300 m (985 ft.). The black line shows the path where the Apollo 12 astronauts explored. It is labeled EVA for Extra Vehicular Activity. Ask students to label as many items as they can on their activity sheets (question 4).

9 **Zoom** in towards the astronaut holding a red flag to see a three-dimensional model of the Lunar Lander. Click on the *YouTube*® link next to the ladder to see a video clip called "Pete Conrad Descends to the Surface."

10 Click on other **camera icons** to see panoramic views. Can students find the American flag?

Exploring Space *(cont.)*

Extension Activities

- It is possible to find a few craters that are still visible on Earth. **Fly to** the following craters on Earth: Meteor Crater, Arizona; Aorounga, Chad; Clearwater Lakes, Canada; Manicouagan Crater, Canada. (**Note:** Some of the craters are filled with water.) Have students describe each crater with three mathematical terms (e.g., diameter, depth, area) and compare the craters on the Moon to those on Earth.

- Use the **navigation tools** to explore one of the other Apollo landing sites. Ask students to write a paragraph about the most interesting features they discover and make a **tour** of the site.

- Use the **planets tool** to travel to Mars and look under the **Mars Gallery layer** for the **Rovers and Landers layer** to see where the rovers Spirit and Opportunity are today. Have students research Mars in Google Earth and compare it to the Moon.

Did You Know?

All the Apollo landing sites are on the near side of the Moon so the astronauts could stay in constant contact with Earth. The first time anyone saw the far side of the Moon with their eyes was on the first mission to orbit the Moon, Apollo 8.

Exploring Space *(cont.)*

Screenshots

Planets tool

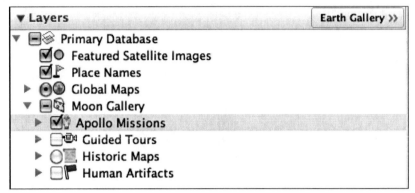

Moon Gallery layer

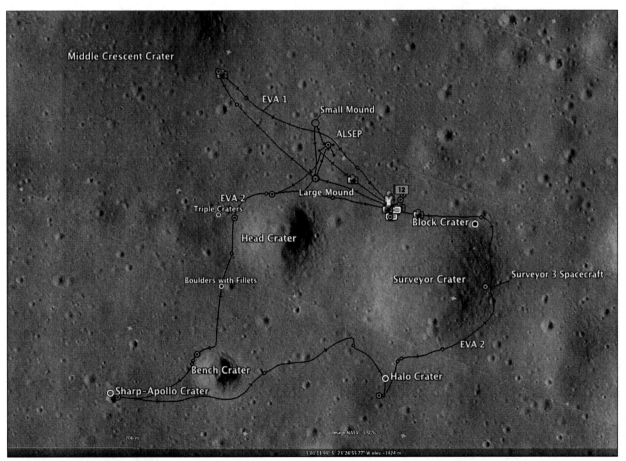

Apollo 12 landing site

Name _____ Date _____

To the Moon

1 Click on the planets tool in the Toolbar and choose Moon. Zoom out as far as you can and rotate the Moon. Describe what you see on the lines below.

_____

_____

_____

2 Placemark Gamow Crater. Use the ruler tool to measure the diameter of Gamow Crater.

diameter = _____

To the Moon *(cont.)*

3 There have been six missions to the Moon. Each mission had three astronauts. In each mission, two astronauts walked on the Moon, and one stayed in the Command Module. The astronauts left their equipment on the Moon to make room in their spaceship for Moon rocks. They even left their boots.

How many pairs of Moon boots are currently on the Moon? _____

Are all the boots in the same place? Why or why not?

_____

_____

4 Zoom in to see the Apollo 12 landing site on the moon (Eye alt about 762 m or 2,500 ft.). On the diagram below, label the features you discover along the Extra Vehicular Activity (EVA) path.

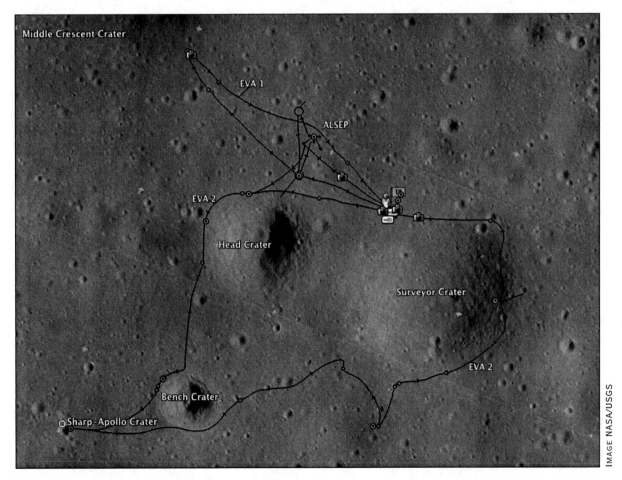

Diving Into the Ocean

Standards

Students know the physical components of Earth's atmosphere, lithosphere, hydrosphere, and biosphere. Students understand ways in which human action has contributed to long-term changes in the natural environments in particular regions or worldwide.

Google Earth Tools

- Layers panel: Borders and Labels
- Layers panel: Oceans: Animal Tracking*
- Status bar: Eye alt
- View: Water Surface*

Overview

Students will explore the ocean by looking at underwater trenches and island formations and by tracking the migration of sea animals.

Vocabulary

- reef
- trench
- seamount

Materials

- *How Deep Is the Ocean?* activity sheets (pages 209–210)
- chart paper

Procedure

1. Ask students what they know about the ocean. Have them describe some features of the ocean and write their ideas on a sheet of chart paper. Distribute copies of the *How Deep Is the Ocean?* activity sheets (pages 209–210) to students and open Google Earth.

2. **Zoom** out as far as possible. Ask students why Earth looks so blue. **Fly to** The Bahamas and **zoom** in to an **Eye alt** of 1,600 km (1,000 mi.). Ask students to answer question 1 on their activity sheets.

3. Turn on the **Borders and Labels layer** in the **Layers panel**. **Fly to** Guam and **zoom** in to the town of Merizo on the southern tip of the island. Navigate to an **Eye alt** of about 9 km (30,000 ft.) to see the tip of the island and the bright blue ocean area to the south. This is a reef that is shallow in the center and bordered by coral. **Zoom** in to the ocean just south of the reef. Notice the waves around the coral reef. This ocean surface is part of an image. If you navigate directly south, you will see the edge of that image. **Zoom** out to an **Eye alt** of about 40 km (25 mi.) and look at the areas outside the image. These areas are animations of the ocean, not images.

* Tool introduced in this lesson

Diving Into the Ocean *(cont.)*

Procedure *(cont.)*

4 **Zoom** to an **Eye alt** of about 1,600 km (1,000 mi.) and point out the Mariana Trench to the east of Guam. Tell students this is the deepest trench in the ocean. Move the cursor over the trench and ask students to use the **elev** display in the **Status bar** to write the depth of the trench on their activity sheets (question 2).

5 **Fly to** Hawaii and **zoom** in to the Big Island of Hawaii at an **Eye alt** of about 130 km (80 mi.). Explore the ocean surface around this island. Make sure the **Borders and Labels layer** is on in the **Layers panel** to see *Loihi Seamount* just to the south of the Big Island (18 54 N 155 16 W).

6 Click on **View** in the **Menu Bar** and select **Water Surface**. This enables you to dive beneath the water surface to explore the ocean. **Zoom** in until you dive below the surface of the ocean to the seamount. Use the **Look joystick** to provide a perspective view of the seamount. Students should see the ocean's surface above and the seamount in perspective. Use the **Look joystick** to look around. Explain to students that a seamount is a volcano that is forming. When it is big enough to rise above the ocean's surface, it will be an island. Have students answer question 3 on their activity sheets.

7 In the **Layers panel** you will see the **Ocean layer**. Many of the layers within this folder lead to places in the ocean and then present pop-up windows with a photograph, some text, and possibly a video. **Fly to** San Diego, California, and **zoom** to an **Eye alt** of about 1,100 km (1,000 mi.). Turn on the **Animal Tracking layer** under the **Oceans layer** in the **Layers panel**. Point out the **animal icons** that appear along the coast of California and Mexico.

8 Click on one of the **animals icons** for information about that sea animal. The pop-up window also includes links that allow the viewer to swim alongside the animal, or, if this animal has been tagged, to track its path in the water. Click **Download track** to see where each animal has traveled.

9 Have students choose an animal and fill in the information in questions 4 and 5 on their activity sheets. Using the ruler tool, students can use the **Path tab** to measure the distance the animal traveled.

Diving Into the Ocean *(cont.)*

Extension Activities

- **Fly to** Monterey, California, and look at the Monterey Submarine Canyon. Have students investigate the depth and compare it to other above-ground canyons, such as the Grand Canyon. Have students dive under the surface and look around this canyon. Ask them to write a short story from the point of view of a sea animal who lives there.

- Read a book about adventures on the ocean, like *Call It Courage* (Sperry 1941), and make a tour of the setting, highlighting features in the ocean or on the islands.

Did You Know?

The Hawaiian Islands were formed when the Pacific plate moved north over a hot spot below the ocean's surface. The first island to form over the hot spot was Kauai. As the plate moved northwest, Oahu, Molokai, and then Maui formed. Now the Big Island of Hawaii is over the hot spot and has active volcanoes, especially Kilauea.

User Tip

In most places, the ocean bottom topography is very low resolution, but around Hawaii, the resolution is high enough to provide an exciting view below the sea surface.

Diving Into the Ocean *(cont.)*

Screenshots

Merizo, Guam

animal icons

Name _____ Date _____

How Deep Is the Ocean?

1 Fly to The Bahamas and zoom out to an Eye alt of 1,600 km (about 1,000 mi.). How many different shades of blue do you see?

_____

Why is some water a lighter blue than the surrounding ocean?

_____

_____

2 What is the depth of the Mariana Trench?

_____

3 Explore underwater around the shorelines of the Big Island of Hawaii. Compare the underwater landscape to the above-ground landscape. Name two ways they are the same and two ways they are different.

_____

_____

_____

_____

_____

How Deep Is the Ocean? *(cont.)*

 4   Turn on the Animal Tracking layer and choose an animal to follow by clicking on one of the icons. Answer the following questions about your animal, then share what you found with the class.

Write a brief description of the animal.

_____

_____

Where does this animal live?

_____

How far did this animal travel?

_____

Does this animal prefer deep or shallow water?

_____

5   *Challenge:* Why do some animals travel long distances, while others stay in one location?

_____

_____

_____

_____

Imagining Places

Google Earth Tools
- Layers panel: 3D Buildings
- Street View*

Overview
Students will investigate the possible locations of imaginary places from fiction.

Vocabulary
- genre
- scouts

Materials
- *Where in the World...?* activity sheets (pages 214–216)

Procedure

1 Ask students if they have ever read any of the *Harry Potter* books by J.K. Rowling, or other book series that takes place in an imaginary place. Ask students if the places in the story are real or imaginary (e.g., *Hogwarts and Diagon Alley are imaginary but London is real*).

2 Tell students that movie location scouts are people who look for locations to film movies that match what the author has described in a book. The scouts for the *Harry Potter* movies chose England and Scotland for most of the filming.

3 Distribute copies of the *Where in the World...?* activity sheets (pages 214–216) to students and open Google Earth.

4 Much of the action of the Harry Potter stories takes place at Hogwarts Castle. There is no such place in real life, but students can see the castle that is used in some scenes in the movies. **Fly to** Edinburgh Castle, Edinburgh, Scotland. Click and hold on the **pegman icon** (between the **Move joystick** and the **zoom slider**) until you see blue lines on the roads. Drag the **pegman icon** and drop it anywhere with the blue lines to enter **Street View** and look around. Have students record what they see on their activity sheets (question 1).

* Tool introduced in this lesson

Imagining Places *(cont.)*

Procedure *(cont.)*

5 Then, **Fly to** the Elephant House, Edinburgh, and use the **pegman icon** to enter **Street View**. The cafe is where J.K. Rowling wrote much of the Harry Potter series. Navigate to Candlemaker Row and Merchant Street (55 56 51.14 N 3 11 32.39 W) and look at the view of Edinburgh Castle from the back window of the Elephant Cafe.

6 **Fly to** two other imaginary locations from the book series of your choice. Click on the **3D Buildings layer** in the **Layers panel** to get a closer look at these locations. If you are using the *Harry Potter* series, explore Glenfinian Viaduct in Scotland (56 52 34 N 5 25 52 W), the bridge the Hogwarts Express travels over in the films, or King's Cross Station in London, England with these features.

7 Explain that the *Harry Potter* stories are fantasy stories, which is one kind of genre. Have students write a definition for the fantasy genre by listing some of the characteristics of a fantasy story, and then thinking of some appropriate settings (question 2). For example, if fantasy stories usually have magical creatures, where would those creatures need to live? If fantasy stories usually include kings or queens, where would they need to live?

8 Have students describe the characteristics of the different genres listed on their activity sheets (question 3). Then, **Fly to** the locations listed and match each location to one of the genres (question 4). Have students explain why they chose to match the setting to that genre.

Extension Activities

- *Lord of the Rings* (Tolkien 1965) was filmed in New Zealand in a variety of locations. **Fly to** Hobbiton Movie Set and Farm Tours, Matamata, New Zealand. Turn on the **Photos layer** and look one mile north to see photos of the hobbit homes.

- Use **Street View** to look at your school. Have students write a letter to the director of an imaginary film, arguing why your school is a perfect filming location.

Imagining Places *(cont.)*

Did You Know? ✕

Some fantasy stories, like *Star Wars*, take place in the desert. An unusual desert used to film some scenes is Chott el Djerid, Nefta, Tunisia.

Screenshot

Edinburgh Castle 3D model

©2011 GETMAPPING PLC

Name _____ Date _____

Where in the World...?

1 Look around Edinburgh Castle and record your observations below.

_____

_____

_____

_____

2 On the lines below, describe some characteristics of a fantasy story.

_____

_____

_____

_____

Now list some possible locations for fantasy stories based on the qualities you described.

_____   _____

_____   _____

_____   _____

Where in the World...? *(cont.)*

3 List two characteristics of each of the genres shown below.

Western: _____   _____

Science fiction: _____   _____

Pirates: _____   _____

Fairy tale: _____   _____

Mystery: _____   _____

Action/Adventure: _____   _____

Futuristic: _____   _____

4 Fly to the locations below. Describe the genre that would best be associated with the location and explain why you chose that genre.

- Tortuga, Haiti

  Genre: _____

  Why: _____

  _____

- Devil's Tower National Monument, Wyoming

  Genre: _____

  Why: _____

  _____

Where in the World...? *(cont.)*

 5 Fly to the locations below. Describe the genre that would best be associated with the location and explain why you chose that genre.

- Tongariro National Park, New Zealand

    Genre: _____

    Why: _____

    _____

- Monument Valley, Arizona

    Genre: _____

    Why: _____

    _____

- Neuschwanstein Castle, Bavaria, Germany

    Genre: _____

    Why: _____

    _____

- Eden Project, Cornwall, United Kingdom

    Genre: _____

    Why: _____

    _____

- Alcatraz, California

    Genre: _____

    Why: _____

    _____

Drawing on Earth

Standard
Students understand connections among the various art forms and other disciplines.

Google Earth Tools

- Layers panel: Photos
- Layers panel: More: Wikipedia
- Layers panel: Gallery: YouTube*
- View: Scale Legend

Overview

Students will see art on Earth and then create a myth inspired by images in Google Earth.

Vocabulary

- geoglyphs
- Nazca Lines
- texture

Materials

- *Ancient Drawings* activity sheets (pages 220–222)
- crayons or markers
- paper

* Tool introduced in this lesson

Procedure

1 Viewing Earth from above lets us see the many colors, shapes, and textures of our planet—both natural and artificial or man-made. One particular example of this is the discovery of the Nazca Lines in Peru—patterns drawn on the desert between 500 B.C. and 500 A.D. that were not discovered until the 1930s when airplanes began flying over them.

2 Distribute copies of the *Ancient Drawings* activity sheets (pages 220–222) to students and open Google Earth.

3 **Fly to** Nazca Lines, Peru, and **zoom** in to about 600 m (2,000 ft.). Ask students if they see anything in the **3D viewer** that looks like it is an artificial feature. Have them draw what they see on their activity sheets (question 1).

4 **Zoom** out to about 4 km (13,000 ft.). To get an idea of what the lines look like from an airplane, turn on the **YouTube layer** in the **Gallery layer** and click the **YouTube icon** titled "Peru, Nazca Lines" to play the video.

5 In the **Layers panel**, open the **More layer** and then turn on the **Wikipedia layer**. **Zoom** out until you see the **Wikipedia icon**. Click on it and read about the geoglyphs (lines). Have students write a definition for geoglyph on their activity sheets (question 2).

Drawing on Earth *(cont.)*

Procedure *(cont.)*

Turn off all layers except the **Photos layer** and **zoom** to an **Eye alt** of about 8 km (27,000 ft.). **Panoramio™ icons** will appear over some of the more famous lines. Click on a **Panoramio icon**, and then click on the image in the **Panoramio window** to see what the lines look like in each area. Return to Google Earth and **zoom** over the other **Panoramio™ icons** to find the other Nazca Lines. Have students write the patterns they see on their activity sheets (question 3).

Use a **Scale Legend** (see the *Creating Reference Scales* lesson, pages 73–76) to determine the relative sizes of these images.

8 Tell students that there are more locations on Earth with art that was created more recently. **Fly to** the locations listed on the activity sheets (question 4) and ask students to describe the Earth art they see. Ask students to make a guess as to how each image was created.

9 Ask students to choose one Earth art pattern or to invent a pattern of their own and write a myth about the figure they chose (question 5).

Extension Activities

- The colors visible on Earth from space can create dramatic and artistic views. Tell students to look at the locations from the list below. Have them write down the colors they see and have them describe what is creating those colors (e.g., water, snow, vegetation, desert soil).

  ➤ Lake Carnegie, Australia

  ➤ Pandacan, Manila, Philippines

  ➤ Male, North Central Province, Maldives

  ➤ Leona River, Santa Cruz Province, Argentina

- Textures visible on Earth from space can create dramatic and artistic views. Tell students to look at the locations from the list below. Have them write down the textures they see and have them describe what is creating those textures.

  ➤ Tien Shan, China

  ➤ Atlas Mountains, Algeria

  ➤ Timbuktu, Mali

Drawing on Earth *(cont.)*

Did You Know? ⊗

Close-ups of the Nazca Lines indicate that the rust-colored rocks were removed to expose the light-colored lime rock surface below.

"Earth art" is an art form that is created in nature using natural materials, such as rock, logs, soil, and water, along with man-made materials such as concrete and metal. The works are usually in the open and are left to erode over time.

Screenshot

IMAGE ©2011 DIGITALGLOBE, ©2011 TELE ATLAS

Nazca Lines, Peru

Name _____ Date _____

Ancient Drawings

 1 Fly to Nazca Lines, Peru. Draw what you see in the space below and describe it on the lines below.

_____

_____

_____

_____

2 Write a definition for *geoglyph* in your own words.

_____

_____

_____

_____

Ancient Drawings *(cont.)*

3 On the lines below, describe some of the Nazca Lines images you see:

_____

_____

_____

_____

4 Fly to the locations listed in the first column in the chart below. Describe the image that you see at each location in the third column. In the last column, make a guess about how that image was created.

Location	Directions	Image	How do you think this image was created?
31 59 20 S 152 34 18 E	Eye alt 1 km or 3,500 ft.		
54 13 29 N 1 12 44 W	Eye alt 1 km or 3,500 ft.		
44 14 39 N 7 46 10 E	Eye alt 2 km or 7,000 ft.		

Ancient Drawings *(cont.)*

5 Choose one Nazca pattern and write a myth about how and why these lines were drawn in the desert.

_____

_____

_____

_____

_____

_____

_____

_____

_____

_____

_____

_____

_____

References Cited

Bean, T. 2010. *Multimodal learning for the 21st century adolescent.* Huntington Beach, CA: Shell Education.

Card, S. K., J. D. Mackinlay, and B. Shneiderman. 1999. *Readings in information visualization: Using vision to think.* San Francisco, CA: Morgan Stanley Kaufmann Publishers.

Castiglione, C. 2009. New media project: Information visualization. Unpublished report.

Common Core State Standards for English Language Arts. 2010. http://www.corestandards.org/the-standards/ Accessed August 25, 2011.

Conklin, W. 2007. *Applying differentiation strategies.* Huntington Beach, CA: Shell Education.

———. 2011. *Activities for a differentiated classroom.* Huntington Beach, CA: Shell Education.

Frei, S., A. Gammill, and S. Irons. 2007. *Integrating technology into the curriculum.* Huntington Beach, CA: Shell Education.

Image Science and Analysis Laboratory, NASA-Johnson Space Center. "The Gateway to Astronaut Photography of Earth." http://eol.jsc.nasa.gov. Accessed August 22, 2011.

Maggio, Alice. 2003. Measuring a Chicago mile. Gapers Block: Ask the Librarian. http://www.gapersblock.com/airbags/archives/measuring_a_chicago_mile/. (Oct. 2.)

NASA Earth Observatory. The Earth Observatory Science Project Office. http://earthobservatory.nasa.gov/. Accessed Aug. 22, 2011.

Roschelle, J., R. Pea, C. Headley, D. Gordin, and B. Means. 2001. *Changing what and how children learn in school with computer-based technologies. The Future of Children* 10(2): 76–101.

Science Education Resource Center (SERC). 2009. *Why teach with Google Earth*™? Starting Point: Teaching Entry Level Geoscience. http://serc.carlton.edu. Accessed July 20, 2011.

Shultz, R. B., J. Kerski, and T. Patterson. 2008. *The use of virtual globes as a spatial teaching tool with suggestions for metadata standards.* National Council for Geographic Education. *Journal of Geography* 107: 27–34.

Silverstein, G., J. Frechtling, and A. Miyaoka. 2000. *Evaluation of the use of technology in Illinois public schools: Final report.* Rockville, MB: Westat.

Answer Key

A Look from Above (pages 35–36)

1. Adjectives will vary.

2. Pictures will vary.

3. green   *forest or vegetation*
blue   *bodies of water*
brown   *mountains, land*
tan   *desert*
white   *snow or ice*

4. The horizon shows an eye-level view of the world from the position of standing on Earth.

5. c, b, a

My Community (pages 41–42)

1. 6 circles; 12 squares; 13 rectangles; 11 triangles; other shapes may include star, trapezoid.

2. Responses will vary.

3. Responses will vary.

4. Drawings will vary.

5. Responses will vary.

6. Responses may include buildings, playgrounds, fences, etc.

Placemarking the Pyramids (pages 47–48)

1. Maps key should include a color for the desert, a symbol for the pyramids, and a symbol or color for populated areas; square; 4 sides

2. Placemark should be on the pyramid.

3. Responses may include: The larger pyramids may indicate that men were considered more important than women.

4. Responses may include: suburbs, streets, buildings, swimming pools, parks; green represents vegetation, blue represents water, gray, brown, or tan represent buildings

5. Icons will vary.

6.

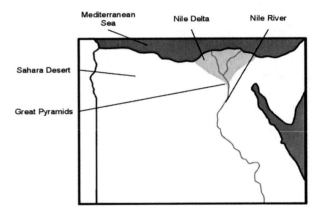

World in 3D (pages 53–54)

1. Definitions may include: a historical structure, a building or structure that marks a boundary or locality.

2. Icons and responses will vary.

3. Responses will vary.

4. Brussels; Berne.

5. Responses will vary.

6. Responses will vary.

Walls All Around (pages 58–60)

1. Natural: palm tree, mountain, Grand Canyon, beach; Artificial: dam, freeway, bridge, fort

2. Responses may be between 64 and 161 km (40 and 100 mi.).

3. Possible response is around 24 km (15 mi.). Astronauts in space most likely cannot view the Great Wall because it is not visible at their distance from Earth.

4. Possible responses include: Xian protected the city's border; Beaumaris protected the king; Plimouth protected the colony.

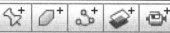

Answer Key *(cont.)*

5. Possible common and different features include: all walls offer protection; the walls at Xian and Beaumaris are thick and have towers; Plimouth's wall is less sturdy.

6. Responses may include: The people in Plimouth at the time did not have access to resources, large numbers of workers, and sophisticated tools to build large walls, as did the people in Xian and Beaumaris.

Elevation Situation (pages 64–66)

1. Plateau
Forest
River
Volcano

2. Responses may include: forest, flatlands, grassy areas, rocks

3. Melting ice; Streams are formed, erosion occurs

4. elevation—the height of land above the level of the sea

5. elevation at top of volcano approx 13,000 km (8,000 ft.)
elevation at park boundary approx 380 m (1,200 ft.)
elevation at sea level 0 m (0 ft.)

6. (elevations are approximate)

Feature	Location	Eye alt	Highest Elevation	Lowest Elevation
mountain	Matterhorn, Italy	6,000 m (20,000 ft.)	4,000 m (14,000 ft.)	0 (at Ligurian Sea)
sea	North Aral Sea, Kazakhstan	3,000 km (200 mi.)	50 m (200 ft.)	40 m (130 ft.)
island	Isla Fernandina, Ecuador	40 km (25 mi.)	1,000 m (4,000 ft.)	0 m (0 ft.)
canyon	Grand Canyon, Arizona	115 km (71 mi.)	1,900 m (6,200 ft.)	880 m (2,900 ft.)

Lines Around Earth (pages 73–74)

1.

2.

3.

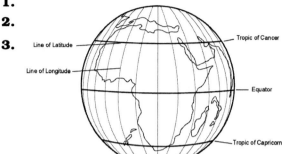

4.

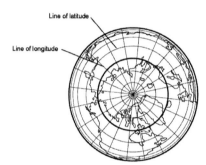

5. Latitude lines are parallel at the pole and longitude lines are intersecting.

6. nevers rises above the horizon or never sets below the horizon.

7. Australia; Sydney; Sydney Harbor Bridge

Answer Key *(cont.)*

Comparing Sizes and Distances (pages 77–78)

1. about 65 m (215 ft.)
2. Responses will vary.
3. Responses will vary.
4. Colosseum, 185 m (610 ft.); Meteor Crater, 1,250 m (4,000 ft.); Uluru, 3,000 m (10,000 ft.); the Sphinx, 74 m (243 ft.); St. Basil's Cathedral, 40 m (130 ft.)

Sorting Our World (pages 83–84)

1. Responses will vary.
2. Responses will vary.

Back in Time (pages 88–90)

1. Labels should include the imaginary character and his/her parents (mother, father) and grandparents (maternal grandmother and grandfather, paternal grandmother and grandfather).
2. Responses will vary.
3. Students should label their own family trees.
4. Responses will vary.
5. Responses will vary.

New York Stories (pages 94–96)

1. Descriptions will vary.
2. Descriptions will vary.
3. Responses will vary.
4. Responses will vary.
5. Descriptions will vary.

A Path Through History (pages 100–102)

1. Responses will vary.
2. Responses will vary; 26
3. Responses will vary.
4. Journal entries will vary.

Customizing Placemarks (pages 106–108)

1. He compared the island to a dolphin.
2. Responses will vary.
3. Responses will vary.
4. Students should circle the first quote.

5.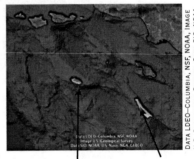
   San Nicolas Santa Catalina
6. Approximately 92 m (57 mi.)
7. No, the distance is too great.

Tracing a Journey (pages 112–114)

1. Students will placemark Boston, Massachusetts; Rio de Janeiro, Brazil; the Straits of Magellan; Coquimbo, Chile; the Galapagos islands, Ecuador; San Francisco, California.
2. Yes, Jack crossed the equator.
3. It got warmer as they neared the equator and cooler as they moved away from the equator.
4. The path is about 24,100 km (15,000 mi.). Yes, because Praiseworthy predicted 15,000 mi.
5. Postcards will vary.

Take Me There (pages 118–120)

1. Timelines will vary.
2. Descriptions will vary.
3. Plans will vary.

Answer Key *(cont.)*

Telling a Story (pages 124–126)

1. Responses will vary.

2. Details will vary.

3. Scripts will vary.

Times Will Change (pages 130–132)

1. Students should write "a" on their birth year and "b" on the year their school was built.

2. It is a similar shape, but the location

is different.

3. November 29, 2006; April 2, 2009

4. Babe Ruth: old; Mickey Mantle: old; Jackie Robinson: old; Derek Jeter: new

5. Old stadium: 121 m (399 ft.); New stadium: 122 m (400 ft.)

6. Possible response: The two towers are gone and have been replaced by a memorial.

Magellan's Journey (pages 136–138)

1. San Lucar de Barameda, inlet; Canarias Islands, island; Rio de Janiero, peninsula; Rio de la Plata, inlet; Port San Julian, inlet; Strait of Magellan, strait; Puka Puka, island; Guam, island; The Phillipines, island.

2. No

3. Yes

4. Responses will vary.

5. An inlet is a passage to an enclosed place; a strait is a narrow stretch of water bounded by land, between two larger bodies of water. An inlet is similar to a strait because they both look like they provide passage through land.

6. Paths will vary.

7. Responses will vary.

Then and Now (pages 142–144)

1. Timeline should be filled in chronologically: 1607 Jamestown is established and Virginia becomes the first colony; 1775 Paul Revere begins his ride; 1776 Declaration of Independence is signed; 1787 Delaware becomes the first state; 1790 Rhode Island is the last colony to become a state; 1804 Lewis and Clark begin their expedition; 1846 The Oregon Trail is in full swing.

2. Responses may include rivers, mountains, or lakes.

3. Responses will vary.

Earthquake Strikes! (pages 149–150)

1. Responses may include parks, cities, or buildings.

2. Responses may include rubble or destruction from the earthquake.

3. Responses may include tent cities or some reconstruction.

4. Responses will vary.

5. Responses will vary.

Runoff Through the Great Lakes (pages 154–156)

1. evaporation—heated water turns to water vapor; condensation—water vapor cools and converts to liquid; precipitation—water falls to Earth as rain, snow, etc.; runoff—water flows downhill toward the ocean

2.

3. Yes; when you zoom in you can see the waterways.

Answer Key *(cont.)*

4. Approximate elevations: Lake Superior, 179 m; Lake Michigan, 175 m; Lake Huron, 175 m; Lake Erie, 172 m; Lake Ontario, 73 m.

5. Elevation of west side of locks: 185 m
Elevation of east side of locks: 179 m
Difference in elevation: 6 m

6. About 1,200 km (770 mi.)

7. 12

8. Approximately 1,600 km (1,000 mi.)

Destructive Volcanoes (pages 161–162)

1. The more recent image is on the right.

2. Responses may include loss of vegetation, dome, craters.

3. About 2 km (1.3 mi.)

4. Oregon

5. No. Responses will vary. Possible response: It is covered in ice, so there is no evidence of an eruption.

Night and Day (pages 166–168)

1. Students should shade the left half of the globe.

2. Arrows should move in the opposite direction from the sun.

3. one minute, one hour, one day, one week, one month, one year

4. Yes, because the poles tilt toward half of the sun for part of the year

5. Students should describe life in constant daylight and constant darkness.

Fuel Sources (pages 173–174)

1. Kentucky, Tennessee, Virginia, West Virginia

2. Responses may include loss of vegetation, loss of wildlife.

3. Characteristics may include mountainous ranges, smoke stacks, barren landscapes around the mines.

4. Drawings will vary.

Washington, DC (pages 178–480)

1. capital—the location of a government in a country or a state

2. Responses may include roads, buildings, monuments, trees, parks.

3. Responses may include stars, triangles, angles, and parallelograms.

4. 110° southwest; 1.6 mi.

5. DuPont Circle 335° NW; 1.5 m (1,750 ft.)
Washington Circle 294° NW; 4.3 km (4,250 ft.)

Lincoln Memorial 232° SW; 1.5 km (4,930 ft.)

Jefferson Memorial 360° S; 1.8 km (6,086 ft.)

6. Capitol Building to Jefferson Memorial: 2.5 km (1.6 mi)
Jefferson Memorial to the White House: 1.8 km (1.1 mi.)

7. should be in the river; built in its current position so it would be on land

Subtracting the Amazon (pages 184–186)

1. Responses may include: patches of missing trees.

2. Responses may include: trees were thick and dense in earlier views.

3. Length: 20.61 mi.; Side: 10.14 mi.; Area: 208.9854 mi.²

4. Responses will vary.

5. Responses will vary.

6. Responses will vary.

7. Responses may include: Accurate estimation requires more information.

Plots of Land (pages 190–192)

Answer Key *(cont.)*

1. Responses may include: random shapes.
2. Squares and rectangles
3. Land was sectioned by set numbers of acres.
4. One square mile
5. $\frac{1}{16}$ of 640 = 40 acres
6. 36 square miles
7.

6	5	4	3	2	1
7	8	9	10	11	12
18	17	16	15	14	13
19	20	21	22	23	24
30	29	28	27	26	25
31	32	33	34	35	36

8. 252nd Street and 398th Avenue
9. About 11 miles
10. about .5 miles per hour; about one day (22 hours)
11. .32 hours

Water All Around (pages 196–198)

1. Circles
2. Responses may include: the sprinkler system waters crops in a circle.
3. Students should build model.
4. Well water comes up through the center pivot pipe and sprays from a radial arm that moves around the field.
5. 440 yd.^{2}
6. 607,904 yd.^{2}
7. 845 yards; 713,687 yd.^{2}

To the Moon (pages 203–204)

1. Responses may include: dark and light areas, craters.
2. Diameter is about 120 km or 54 mi.
3. 24 single boots or 12 pairs; the boots will be wherever the missions landed

4. Head Crater, Bench Crater, Surveyor Crater

How Deep Is the Ocean? (pages 209–210)

1. Responses may include: four or five different shades of blue. It is shallower.
2. About –1.5 km (–30,000 ft.) at its deepest
3. Same: landscapes, mountain ranges; Different: above and below water, rocky or sandy
4. Responses will vary.
5. Responses may include: they are looking for warmer water, they are staying close to a food supply.

Where in the World...? (pages 214–216)

1. Responses may include: parking lots, trees, castle walls are stone or brick.
2. Responses may include: kings and queens, castles, magical creatures, forests; Locations may include: castles, forests, deserts.
3. Characteristics may include: Western—desert, ghost town; Science fiction—space, barren or rocky landscape; Pirates—ocean, island; Fairy Tale—forest, castle; Mystery—graveyard, dark forest, spooky mansion; Action/Adventure—mountains, cliffs, jungle; Futuristic—stark buildings, desert, cities
4. Responses will vary.
5. Responses will vary.

Ancient Drawings (pages 220–222)

1. Responses may include: a bird, a whale, a monkey, or hands.
2. geoglyph—works of art that were made from moving or arranging stones or earth on a landscape
3. Responses may include: Ballena (whale), Astonauta (astronaut), Manos (hands), Mono (monkey), Colibri (hummingbird), and Condor (under the Panoramio for "Nazca Lines").
4. shark, horse, rabbit; responses may include: man-made means.
5. Stories will vary.

Assessment Rubric

Use this chart to assess students' technology skills. An example of how to fill it out has been shown here.

Google Earth Skill Assessment Sample

Name: _____

Skill	Cannot Perform	Can Perform with Assistance	Can Perform Independently	Can Use and Apply in Other Situations	Comments
Placemarking			✔		
Create a Path		✔			
Use Ruler Tool				✔	

Assessment Rubric *(cont.)*

Use this chart to assess students' technology skills. Use the blank lines to customize the chart as you want.

Google Earth Skill Assessment Template

Name: _____

Skill	Cannot Perform	Can Perform with Assistance	Can Perform Independently	Can Use and Apply in Other Situations	Comments

How-to Guide

1. Installing and Opening Google Earth

To install Google Earth, go to http://www.earth.google.com and download the latest version. Look for the *.dmg* file on your desktop and click on it. Follow the installation instructions.

To open Google Earth, click on the application. If a pop-up window appears, close it. A view of Earth appears and you are ready to begin.

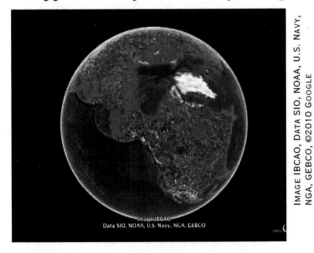

IMAGE IBCAO, DATA SIO, NOAA, U.S. NAVY, NGA, GEBCO, ©2010 GOOGLE

2. Google Earth Window

The **Google Earth Window** includes the **Menu Bar**, the **3D viewer**, the **Toolbar**, and the **Search, Places**, and **Layers Panels**. Within the **3D viewer** are the **Status bar** (at the bottom) and the **navigation tools** (in the upper right). (See page 13 for a full view of the **Google Earth Window** and all the tools, or see Reference.pdf on the Teacher Resource CD.)

3. Google Earth Status Bar

The **Status bar** provides information about the location of the cursor or the center of the **3D viewer**.

Latitude and Longitude: The latitude and longitude (**lat/long**) display in the **Status bar** identifies the coordinates of the cursor, or, if the cursor is off the **3D viewer**, the coordinates at the center of the **3D viewer.**

Elev: The **elev** display represents the elevation, or height of the land relative to sea level at the location of the cursor, or, if the cursor is off the **3D viewer**, the elevation at the center of the **3D viewer.** If the cursor is over the ocean, the elevation is the depth of the ocean.

Eye Alt: **Eye alt** is the height of your eye relative to sea level at the center of the image.

4. Google Earth Navigation Tools

The **navigation tools** allow you to maneuver around the **3D viewer** and to change the **Eye alt** of your view as well as your perspective.

Look Joystick: The **Look joystick** has an eye on it and it allows you to to change your view as if you were moving your eyes. In a close-up view, the arrows allow you to view a mountain or building as if you were standing next to it, looking up and down, left and right. The bottom arrow returns you to an overhead view.

How-to Guide *(cont.)*

The **North-up button** on the **Look joystick** rotates your view clockwise or counterclockwise. When the Earth is not in a North-up view, click the N on the **North-up button** once to return the Earth to a North-up orientation.

Move Joystick: From a close-up view, the **Move joystick** allows you to move to the north, south, east or west of your current view, depending on which arrow you press. Hold down a section of the circle in the **Move joystick** to fly along above Earth. From a global view, the **Move joystick** rotates the Earth around an axis.

Zoom Slider: The **zoom slider** allows you to change your **Eye alt**, which makes it look like you are zooming in and out of a scene in the **3D viewer.** Click and hold on the **+zoom** to move closer to the surface, or the **–zoom** to move farther away.

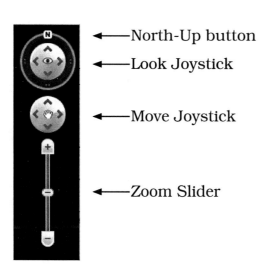

←——North-Up button

←——Look Joystick

←——Move Joystick

←——Zoom Slider

Street View: **Street view** allows you to view a region from the level of the street in some locations. **Zoom** in to an **Eye alt** of between 100 and 500 miles until the **Street View pegman icon** appears above the **zoom slider**. Drag the pegman across the **3D viewer** and look for blue lines. Drop the pegman over any of the blue lines and the view will change to a photograph of the view from the street. Use your cursor to drag the image to the left or right to look around, or use the **Move joystick** to move down the road. (**Note:** This imagery is taken from a camera on top of a car; Google™ is building this data set every day.)

5. Google Earth Search, Places and Layers Panels

Search Panel: Use the **Search panel** to find a specific location. Type the location in the **Fly to box** and click the magnifying glass or the return key on your keyboard. Google Earth recognizes the following types of search terms:

- City, state
- City, country
- Number, street, city, state or country
- Zip code or postal code
- Latitude and longitude (**Note:** These should be entered without symbols, but with spaces between degrees, minutes, seconds and cardinal direction, e.g., 72 33 44 N 134 23 45 E)

How-to Guide *(cont.)*

Sometimes a number of options appear under the **Fly to box**. Double-click the one that you are looking for to fly to it directly.

Places Panel: Places that you have searched for can be dragged from the **Search panel** to the **Places panel** using your cursor. Once in the **Places panel**, these places will appear every time you open Google Earth. **Placemarks**, **paths** and **tours,** as well as folders, are stored in the **Places panel** for future reference.

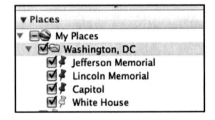

Layers Panel: The **Layers panel** contains a variety of information about Earth in the form of overlays and **placemarks** collected by Google. To see these layers, click the small arrow (Mac) or plus sign (PC) next to **Primary Database** to open the database. Ten layers will appear. Click on the box to the left of each layer turn on the layer and see the overlay or **placemarks** that are contained in that layer. For example, turn on the **Roads layer** to see road lines and names overlaid in Google Earth. When a layer is on, you will see a check mark in the box directly to the left of the layer name. Click the box again to turn the layer off.

If layers have an arrow (Mac) or plus sign (PC) to the left of their names, it means there are additional sublayers available. Click the arrow the plus sign to open the layer menu and see the layers within.

Note: Only keep one or two layers on at a time to prevent Google Earth from slowing down

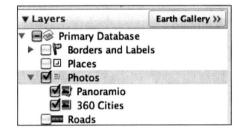

Google Earth is contantly updating the layers data. If any of the layers used in these lessons do not appear in the **Layers panel**, search in the **Google Earth Gallery** for the missing layers.

6. Google Earth Menu Bar

The **Menu Bar**, located at the very top of your computer screen, offers a number of options, some of which are duplicated in the **Toolbar**.

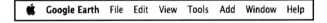

File > Save > Save My Place As: To save a **placemark** or folder, highlight it the **Places panel**. Click **File**, then select **Save** and then **Save My Place As...** to save. A pop-up window will allow you to name the file and

How-to Guide *(cont.)*

choose where to save it. The file is a **.kmz** (keyhole markup language) or **.kml file** named after the computer language used in Google Earth.

Edit > Find: To search for a **placemark** you have previously saved, using a keyword, click **Edit** and select **Find**. In the **Find box** type in a word from the name of a folder or **placemark** that you have saved previously.

View > Grid: To overlay latitude and longitude lines on the Earth, click **View** and select **Grid**. The equator, the Date Line, the Tropics of Cancer and Capricorn, and the Arctic and Antarctic Circles are highlighted.

View > Scale Legend: To add a scale to the lower left corner of the **3D viewer**, click **View** and select **Scale Legend**.

View > Water Surface: To add an artificial water surface over the ocean, click **View** and select **Water Surface**. You can dive below this surface by **zooming** into the ocean and looking up at the surface from below using the **Look joystick**.

7. Google Earth Toolbar

The **Toolbar**, located at the top of the **3D viewer**, allows easy access to a number of tools that can add information to your **3D view**.

Placemark: Save a favorite view as a **placemark** by clicking on the **placemark tool**. In the **Placemark window**, name your **placemark** and add a description. Move the yellow thumbtack cursor in the **3D viewer** to a desired location while the **Placemark window** is open. Click **OK** to save the **placemark**. It will appear either in the **Search panel** or **Places panel**. Drag it to the **Places panel** to save it until the next time you open Google Earth.

To modify or move a **placemark**, right-click (or control-click) on it in the **Places panel**. Select **Get Info** (Mac) or **Properties** (PC) and the **Placemark window** will reappear. You can add a new name or modify the description. Click on the **Style, Color tab** to modify the color and size of the **placemark icon** and label. Choose **View** and use the **navigation tools** to select a new view related to that **placemark**. Click on **Snapshot current view** to keep the new view.

You can change the look of the **placemark icon**. Click on the yellow thumbtack in the upper right corner of the **Placemark window**. A **Placemark icon window** will appear where you can select any number of **placemarks**, or choose **No Icon** if you want to label a **placemark** with a name but not an icon.

How-to Guide *(cont.)*

Placemarks may be collected and organized in folders. At the top of the **Places panel**, right-click (or control-click) on the **My Places** folder and choose **Add**, then **Folder**. **A New Folder window** will appear that is similar to the placemark window. Type in a ame and click OK. This new folder will appear at the bottom of your list of placemarks in the **Places panel**. Move it to the top of the panel just under **My Places** by dragging it with the cursor. Use the cursor to drag placemarks into this folder. Second and third level folders may be added by right clicking on the first level folder, and then proceeding as above.

Polygon: To create a **polygon** around a feature, click on the **polygon tool** and a **polygon window** will appear. Name the **polygon** and move the cursor (which will be a square) to the first corner of the feature you want to label and click once. Click on the next corner and proceed around the area until all corners are clicked. Click on the **Style, Color Tab** in the **polygon window** and choose a color and an opacity for the lines and the area (100% if you want the lines or area to show up; 0% if you want them to disappear). Click OK.

Path: To create a **path**, click on the **Path tool** in the **Toolbar**. You will see a **path window** and a square **path cursor** in the **3D viewer**. Name the **path**. Place the **path cursor** over beginning of your desired path and click once. You should see a colored dot. Now move the cursor along your **path** and click again. The first colored dot will turn a different color, and a new colored dot will appear with a line between the two dots. Click several more times to make a four- or five-point path, then click **OK** to close the path window. A **path placemark** will appear in the **Places panel** (or possibly in the **Search panel**) with a path symbol just to its left.

Note that when the **path window** is open, you will need to navigate using the **navigation tools**. Using the cursor will alter your **path**. If you do this accidentally, you can erase the last point on a path by right clicking (or control-clicking) on it.

Tour: To create a tour of several **placemarks**, organize your **placemarks** according how you want to tour them, and click on the **tour tool** in the **Toolbar**. A **record tour panel** will appear in the lower-left corner of the **3D viewer**. The red button on the left is the start/stop button. The numbers indicate the duration of the tour in minutes and seconds (mm:ss).

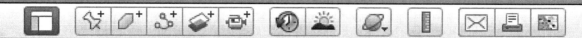

How-to Guide *(cont.)*

To start a **tour**, click on your first **placemark**, and then click the start/stop button on the **record tour panel**. The entire button will turn red. Wait a second and then double-click on the second **placemark** in your tour. The **3D viewer** will navigate to this placemark. Double-click the third **placemark** and the **3D viewer** will go to this place. Continue to the last **placemark**, then click the start/stop button to stop the **tour**.

A **play tour panel** will appear and the **tour** will automatically start playing. The **play tour panel** includes (from the left) *play, pause, go back, and fast-forward* buttons, a tour slider, an indicator of the current time of the **tour,** a repeat button and a save button. Click the save button to save the **tour**.

Clock: The **clock tool** allows you to look at historical imagery that can go back as far as the 1940s in some locations. Click on the **clock tool** in the **Toolbar** and a **timeline slider** will appear in the upper-left corner of the **3D viewer**. Each vertical bar represents an image that was taken in the past. Use the cursor to move the marker along the **timeline slider** to see these historical images.

Sun: Usually the Earth in the **3D viewer** is entirely lit by the **Sun**. To add a shadow representing the night half of the **Earth**, click on the **sun tool** in the **Toolbar**. A **sun slider** will appear in the upper left corner of the **3D viewer**. Move the slider backwards and forwards to follow the shadows on Earth. Click once on the *sun slider* icon that looks like a magnifying glass with a (–) on it. Notice the time span that is being measured changes (one day, one week, one month, one year). Click on the **sun slider play button** (it looks like a clock with an arrow on it) to watch Earth rotate through the time span on the **sun slider.**

Note that in Google Earth, it appears as though the Sun revolves around Earth, when in reality, Earth revolves around the Sun in a year and rotates around its own axis in a day.

Planets: Uncheck all boxes in your **My Places** folder, as well as any open layers in the **Layers panel**. Click on the **planet** icon in the **Toolbar**. Choose *Moon* or *Mars* and proceed to explore these planets as you did Earth. Note that the layers available in the **Layers** panel have changed and allow you to explore the Apollo landing sites for the Moon, and the rover paths for Mars, as well as many other layers.

How-to Guide *(cont.)*

Ruler: To measure a feature in the **3D viewer**, click on the **ruler tool** in the **Toolbar**. In the **Ruler window**, choose your units of length from the drop down menu. Click from one end of a feature you want to measure to the other. A dot will appear at the first click, and as you move the cursor, a yellow line will appear until your next click. The value for length in the **Ruler window** changes as you move the length of the line.

The **ruler tool** also measures heading (an angular direction relative to north). Click on the **Path tab** in the **Ruler window** to measure the length of a **path**.

Email: A view, folder, or **placemark** can be emailed by clicking on the **email tool** in the **Toolbar**. Choose **Graphic of 3D View** to send a *.jpg* image of the current view. Choose **Snapshot of 3D View** to send a **.kmz file**. Choose **Selected Placemark/Folder** to send a **.kmz file** of a selected **placemark** or folder. Click **OK** and you will be directed to your email application. *Note:* In advance of using the **email tool**, you will need to go to **Preferences** under Google Earth in the **Menu Bar**, and select your email program under the **General tab**.

Print: To print an image from Google Earth, go to the **print tool** in the **Toolbar**. Choose **Graphic of 3D View** and then **Screen**, **Low**, or **Medium** to choose the resolution of your print. Then click **Print**. *Note:* The dimensions next to the print options depend on the dimensions of the **Google Earth Window** open on your screen. Note that printing can be very expensive due to the cost of ink.

Google Earth Skills Matrix

Activity Title	Google Earth Skill Used
Flying and Finding Earth (page 31)	• **3D viewer** • **Look joystick** • **Move joystick** • **Search, Places, and Layers panels** • **North-up button** • **Zoom slider**
Searching to Find Me (page 37)	• **Search panel: Fly to box**
Saving Your Place (page 43)	• **Toolbar: Placemark**
Exploring with Layers (page 49)	• **Layers panel: Borders and Labels** • **Layers panel: Photos** • **Layers panel: 3D Buildings** • **Layers panel: More: Wikipedia** • **Places panel: My Places folder** • Toolbar: Placemark
Identifying Artificial Features (page 55)	• **Layers panel: Places** • Toolbar: Placemark • Places panel: My Places folder • **Status bar: Eye alt**
Investigating Natural Features (page 61)	• **Status bar: elev** • Status bar: Eye alt • **Toolbar: Clock** • Toolbar: Placemark
Overlaying Abstract Features (page 67)	• Layers panel: Borders and Labels, Places • Status bar: Eye alt • **Status bar: lat/long** • **View: Grid**
Creating Reference Scales (page 73)	• Toolbar: Placemark • **Toolbar: Ruler** • **View: Scale Legend**
Sorting Our Folders (page 79)	• **Toolbar: Placemark: Find** • **Places panel: Folders**

Note: Bold indicates the lesson in which a tool is introduced and in which directions for its use are included.

Google Earth Skills Matrix *(cont.)*

Activity Title	Google Earth Skill Used
Following Our Family Trees (page 85)	• Places panel: Folders • Toolbar: Placemark
Making Literature Connections (page 91)	• **File: Save: Save Place As...** • Layers panel: 3D Buildings • **Layers panel: Roads** • Places panel: Folders • Toolbar: Placemark
Building History Connections (page 97)	• Status bar: Eye alt • Toolbar: Placemark
Mapping the Plot of a Book (page 103)	• Layers panel: Borders and Labels • Status bar: Eye alt • **Toolbar: Placemark with Description and View** • Toolbar: Ruler
Following the Path of a Book (page 109)	• Toolbar: Placemark • **Toolbar: Path**
Touring a Book (page 115)	• Toolbar: Placemark • **Toolbar: Tour**
Creating a Book Report (page 121)	• **Toolbar: Placemark: Style, Color** • **Toolbar: Tour: Audio**
Going Back in Time (page 127)	• **Toolbar: Clock**
Following Explorers (page 133)	• **.kmz files** • Toolbar: Path, Placemark
Mapping History (page 139)	• Layers panel: Borders and Labels • **Layers panel: Gallery: Rumsey Historical Maps** • Toolbar: Placemark
Tracking the News (page 145)	• **Layers panel: Gallery: Earthquakes** • Status bar: Eye alt • Toolbar: Clock, Ruler
Understanding the Water Cycle (page 151)	• Status bar: elev • Status bar: Eye alt • Toolbar Ruler

Google Earth Skills Matrix *(cont.)*

Activity Title	Google Earth Skill Used
Discovering Forces of Change (page 157)	• .kmz files • Layers panel: Borders and Labels • **Layers panel: Gallery: Coastlines, Volcanoes** • **Places panel: Places slider** • **Places panel: Temporary Places folder** • Toolbar: Placemark, Ruler
Shading the Earth (page 163)	• **Toolbar: Sun**
Using Energy (page 169)	• **Layers panel: Global Awareness: Appalachian Mountaintop Removal** • Layers panel: Borders and Labels, Roads • Places panel: Temporary Places folder • Toolbar: Placemark
Building a Capital (page 175)	• Status bar: Eye alt • Toolbar: Placemark • **Toolbar: Ruler: Heading**
Estimating Deforestation (page 181)	• Status bar: Eye alt • Toolbar: Clock, Ruler • **Toolbar: Polygon**
Measuring America (page 187)	• **Layers panel: More: Transportation: Rail** • Layers panel: Roads • Status bar: Eye alt • Toolbar: Polygon, Ruler
Designing Crops (page 193)	• Places panel: Places slider • Status bar: Eye alt • **Toolbar: Image Overlay** • Toolbar: Ruler
Exploring Space (page 199)	• **Layers panel: Moon Gallery: Apollo Missions** • Places panel: My Places folder • Status bar: Eye alt • Toolbar: Placemark, Ruler • **Toolbar: Planets**
Diving Into the Ocean (page 206)	• Layers panel: Borders and Labels • **Layers panel: Oceans: Animal Tracking** • Status bar: Eye alt • **View: Water Surface**

Google Earth Skills Matrix *(cont.)*

Activity Title	Google Earth Skill Used
Imagining Places (page 211)	• Layers panel: 3D Buildings • **Street View**
Drawing on Earth (page 217)	• Layers panel: Photos • Layers panel: More: Wikipedia • **Layers panel: Gallery: YouTube** • View: Scale Legend

Recommended Literature

Learning to Fly

Flying and Finding Earth

Arthus-Bertrand, Yann. *Earth From Above*. New York: Harry N. Abrams, 2010.

Arthus-Bertrand, Yann. *Earth From Above for Young Readers*. New York: Harry N. Abrams, 2002.

Saving Your Place

Charman, Andrew. *Life and Times in Ancient Egypt*. New York: Kingfisher, 2007.

Smith, Miranda. *Curious Kids: Ancient Egypt*. New York: Kingfisher, 2002.

Stanley, Diane. *Cleopatra*. Madison: Demco Media, 1997.

Exploring with Layers

Hugo, Victor. *Classic Starts: The Hunchback of Notre-Dame*. New York: Sterling Publishing Company, 2008.

Hugo, Victor. *The Hunchback of Notre Dame (Great Illustrated Classics)*. Edina: Abdo Publishing Company, 2002.

Seeing Earth

Identifying Artificial Features

Mahy, Margaret. *The Seven Chinese Brothers*. New York: Scholastic, 1990.

Riggs, Kate. *Great Wall of China*. Mankato, MN Creative Education, 2009.

Sis, Peter. *Tibet Through the Red Box*. New York: Farrar, Straus and Giroux, 1998.

Investigating Natural Features

Kalman, Bobbie and Macaulay, Kelley. *Introducing Landforms (Looking at Earth)*. New York: Crabtree Publishing, 2008.

Publishing, Dorling Kindersley. *Geography of the World*. New York: DK Children, 2006.

Rissman, Rebecca. *What Is a Landform?*. Chicago: Heinemann Raintree Classroom, 2009.

Overlaying Abstract Features

Chesanow, Neil. *Where Do I Live?*. Hauppauge: Barron's Educational Books, 1995.

Ritchie, Scot. *Follow That Map!: A First Look at Mapping Skills*. Tonawanda: Kids Can Press Ltd., 2009.

Sweeney, Dennis. *Me on the Map*. New York: Random House Children's Books, 1998.

Creating Reference Scales

Banyai, Istvan. *Zoom*. London: Puffin Books, 1998.

Building My World

Sorting Our Folders

Silverstein, Shel. *The Poet Tree*. Santa Barbara: Teacher Ideas Press, 1993.

Recommended Literature *(cont.)*

Following Our Family Trees

Rylant, Cynthia. *Henry and Mudge in the Family Trees*. New York: Aladdin Paperbacks, 1998.

Rylant, Cynthia. *The Relatives Came*. Pine Plains: Live Oak Media, 2004.

Say, Allen. *Grandfather's Journey*. Orlando: Houghton Mifflin Harcourt, 1993.

Sweeney, Joan. *Me and My Family Tree*. New York: Random House Children's Books, 2000.

Making Literature Connections

Barrie, James. *Peter Pan*. New York: Penguin Books, 2004.

Bond, Michael. *A Bear Called Paddington*. New York: William Collins and Sons, 1958.

De Angeli, Marguerite. *The Door in the Wall: A Play*. New York: Doubleday, 1949.

Doyle, Adrian. *The Original Illustrated Sherlock Holmes*. Castle Books, 1976.

Rowling, J. K. *Harry Potter and the Sorcerer's Stone*. Farmington Hills: Large Print Press, 2003.

Steinbeck, John. *Of Mice and Men*. New York: Penguin, 1937.

Travers, Pamela. *Mary Poppins*. Louisville: American Printing House for the Blind, 1934.

Building History Connections

D'Aulaire, Ingri and D'Aulaire, Edgar. *Columbus*. New York: Random House Children's Books, 1992.

Sis, Peter. *Follow the Dream: The Story of Christopher Columbus*. New York: Knopf Books for Young Readers, 2003.

Language Arts

Mapping the Plot of a Book

O'Dell, Scott. *Island of the Blue Dolphins*. Orlando: Houghton Mifflin, 1960.

Following the Path of a Book

Fleischman, Sid. *By the Great Horn Spoon!* New York: Little, Brown Books for Young Readers, 1965.

Touring a Book

Fleischman, Sid. *By the Great Horn Spoon!* New York: Little, Brown Books for Young Readers, 1965.

Creating a Book Report

Fleischman, Sid. *By the Great Horn Spoon!* New York: Little, Brown Books for Young Readers, 1965.

Social Studies

Going Back in Time

Curlee, Lynn. *Ballpark: The Story of America's Baseball Fields*. New York: Simon and Schuster, 2005.

Curtis, Arline. *The Little Chapel That Stood*. Escondido: Oldcastle Publishing, 2003.

Englar, Mary. *September 11*. Mankato: Compass Point Books, 2007.

Recommended Literature *(cont.)*

Santella, Andrew. *September 11, 2001.* New York: Scholastic Library Pub, 2007.

Following Explorers

Bailer, Katharine. *Ferdinand Magellan: Circumnavigating the World.* New York: Crabtree Publishing. New York: Grosset and Dunlap, 2005.

Kramer, Sydelle. *Who Was Ferdinand Magellan?.* New York: Grosset and Dunlap, 2004.

Waldman, Stuart. *Magellan's World (Great Explorers).* New York: Mikaya Press, 2007.

Mapping History

Brown, Tricia. *City by the Bay: A Magical Journey Around San Francisco.* San Francisco: Chronicle Books, 1998.

Levick, Melba. *The Missions of California.* San Francisco: Chronicle Books, 2004.

Sasek, Miroslav. *This Is San Francisco.* Kansas City: Universe Press, 2003.

Tracking the News

Stengel, Richard. *Time® for Kids Magazine.* New York: Time Magazine, 1923.

Science

Understanding the Water Cycle

Holling, Holling. *Paddle-to-the-Sea.* Orlando: Houghton Mifflin Harcourt, 1941.

Discovering Forces of Change

Morris, Neil. *Volcanoes.* New York: Crabtree Publishing, Co., 1995.

Rose, Susana. *Volcano and Earthquake.* New York: DK Publishing, Inc., 2008.

Shading the Earth

Branley, Franklyn. *Sunshine Makes the Seasons.* New York: HarperCollins, 2005.

Dayrell, Elphinstone. *Why the Sun and the Moon Live in the Sky.* London: Sandpiper, 1990.

Using Energy

Rockwell, Anne. *What's So Bad About Gasoline?: Fossil Fuels and What They Do.* Pittsburg: Paw Prints Press, 2009.

Woodward, John. *Climate Change.* New York: DK Publishing, 2008.

Zappa, Marcia. *Fossil Fuels (Planet Earth).* Edina: Abdo Publishing Company, 2010.

Mathematics

Building a Capital

Marciano, John. *Madeline at the White House.* New York: Penguin Group USA, 2011.

Obama, Barack. *Of Thee I Sing: A Letter to My Daughters.* New York: Alfred A. Knopf Books for Young Readers, 2010.

Recommended Literature *(cont.)*

Estimating Deforestation

Lynne, Cherry and Plotkin, Mark. *The Sharman's Apprentice*. London: Sandpiper, 2001.

Seuss, Dr. *The Lorax*. New York: Random House Books for Young Readers, 1971.

Beyond Earth

Exploring Space

Chaikin, Andrew and Bean, Alan. *Mission Control this Is Apollo*. New York: Viking Juvenile, 2009.

Floca, Brian. *Moonshot: The Flight of Apollo 11*. New York: Atheneum Books for Young Readers, 2009.

Light, Michael. *Full Moon*. New York: A. A. Knopf, 1999.

Diving Into the Ocean

Heyerdahl, Thor. *Kon Tiki*. Chicago: Rand McNally, 1950.

Kipling, Rudyard. *Captains Courageous*. New York: McMillan & Co., 1897.

O' Dell, Scott. *Black Pearl*. Orlando: Houghton Mifflin Harcourt, 1967.

Sperry, Armstrong. *Call it Courage*. New York: McMillan Press, 1941

Stevenson, Robert. *Treasure Island*. New York: Little, Brown and Company, 1883.

Imagining Places

Baum, L. Frank. *The Wonderful Wizard of Oz*. Chicago: George M. Hill Company, 1900.

Rowling, J.K. *Harry Potter and the Sorcerer's Stone*. New York: Scholastic, 2001.

Tolkien, J.R.R. *The Lord of the Rings*. New York: Ballantine Books, 1954.

Drawing on Earth

Arthus-Bertrand, Yann. *Earth From Above*. New York: Harry N. Abrams, 2010.

Arthus-Bertrand, Yann. *Earth From Above for Young Readers*. New York: Harry N. Abrams, 2002.

Glossary of Terms

agriculture—the science or practice of farming

altitude—height above sea level

archipelago—a chain or cluster of islands

asteroids—small bodies usually composed of rock and/or metal which orbit the sun

axis—a straight line about which a body or geometric object rotates

barren—too poor to produce much or any vegetation

blast zone—area where the blast from an eruption blew over trees

capital—the location of the government of a country or state

capitol—the building in which the government meets

cathedral—a large, important church

category—a class or division of people or things regarded as having particular shared characteristics

characteristic—a distinguishing feature or quality

co-registered—matched

compass rose—a circle or decorative device printed on a map or chart showing the points of the compass

conflict—a serious disagreement or argument

construction—the process of building something

crater—a large, bowl-shaped cavity on the surface of a planet or moon caused by the impact of a meteorite or asteroid

decade—a 10-year period

deforestation—the action of clearing an area of forest

delta—a sediment-filled landform at the mouth of a river where that river water flows over the land

demolish—to destroy or ruin

diameter—a straight line passing from side to side through the center of a circle

elevation—height above sea level

epicenter—the area of Earth's surface directly above the place of origin, or focus, of an earthquake

erode—gradually wear away

erosion—the processes that break down rocks (weathering) and the processes that carry away the breakdown products

floodplain—flat land adjacent to a river that stretches from the banks of the river to the base of the enclosing valley walls, and experiences flooding during high water

fossil fuels—a fuel such as coal or gas, formed in the geological past from the remains of living organisms

genre—a category of artistic composition, as in music or literature, characterized by similarities in form, style, or subject matter

geoglyphs—a drawing on the ground, or a large motif, or design produced on the ground

Glossary of Terms *(cont.)*

geometric—employing simple lines or figures such as circles, squares, triangles, or rectangles

heading—an angular direction relative to north

horizon—the apparent line in the distance where the sky meets the sea or land

horizontal—going straight across from side to side

inlet—a small body of water leading inland from the ocean

intensity—exceptionally great concentration, power, or force

irrigation—supplying dry land with water by means of ditches and pipes

island—a piece of land surrounded by water

journey—an act of traveling from one place to another

kelp—a large brown seaweed growing off the bottom of the sea and often extending to the surface

landmark—a well-known building or natural feature

landscape—a picture representing a view of natural inland scenery

latitude—the visible features of an area of land, including landforms, water bodies, land cover, and man-made structures

locks—a device for raising and lowering boats between stretches of water of different levels on river and canals

longitude—the angular distance of a place east or west of the meridian

magma—fluid or semifluid material below or within Earth's crust from which lava and other igneous rock is formed by cooling

mare—a large, level basalt plain on the surface of the Moon, appearing dark by contrast with highland areas

maternal—relating to or characteristic of a mother or motherhood

mission—a space-based satellite built for a specific purpose, such as taking the images that make up Google Earth

mosaicked—attached together to form a picture or pattern like a puzzle

mudflow zone—area where volcanic mud flowed down a mountain

narrate—provide a spoken commentary to accompany a movie, broadcast, piece of music, etc.

navigate—to direct the movement (of the Google Earth view in this case)

Nazca Lines—large animal and abstract geoglyphs made from rocks in a desert in northern Peru

nonrenewable—natural resources that cannot be replaced by natural processes

parallel—lying in the same direction and always the same distance apart

paternal—relating to or characteristic of a father or fatherhood

peninsula—a piece of land that projects into a body of water and is connected with the mainland

Glossary of Terms *(cont.)*

plot—the main storyline of a literary or dramatic work

pivot—the central point on which a mechanism turns

portage—the carrying of a boat or its cargo between two navigable waters

radius—a straight line from the center to the circumference of a circle or sphere

realistic—representing familiar things in a way that is accurate or true to life

reef—coral feature lying beneath the surface of the water

reference—source of information, something to compare to

renewable—natural resources capable of being replaced by natural processes

revolve—to move in an orbit

rotate—to turn about an axis

runoff—water flow that occurs when soil is saturated and there is excess water from rain and melt

scale—relative size of something

scouts—people who find locations to film movies

seamount—an underwater mountain rising from the ocean floor and having a summit below the surface of the sea

section—a one-mile-by-one-mile plot of land

setting—a story's time and place

strait—a narrow passage of water connecting two seas or large areas of water

structure—something that is built by people, like a building or a bridge

survey—to measure and map the land

texture—the feel, appearance, or consistency of a surface or a substance

timeline—a graphic representation of the passage of time as a line

topography—the 3D arrangement of the terrain

trench—depression in the ocean bottom created at the boundary between two tectonic plates

tropical—a dense forest occurring in the tropics, or near the Equator

tsunami—a long, high sea wave caused by an earthquake or other disturbance in the ocean

vertical—running straight up and down

visible—able to be seen, exposed to view, not hidden

volcano—a rupture in a planet's surface that allows hot magma, ash, and gases to escape from below the surface

wilderness—an area where there are few people living; an area still in its natural state

Contents of Teacher Resource CD

Teacher Resources	
Resource	**File Name**
Recommended Literature	Literature.pdf
Google Earth Reference Window	Reference.pdf
How-to Guide	How_to.pdf
Assessment Rubric for Technology Skills	Tech_Rubric.pdf
Student Activity Sheets	
Learning to Fly	
A Look From Above	page35.pdf
My Community	page41.pdf
Placemarking the Pyramids	page47.pdf
World in 3D	page53.pdf
Seeing Earth	
Walls All Around	page58.pdf
Elevation Situation	page64.pdf
Lines Around Earth	page71.pdf
Comparing Sizes and Distances	page77.pdf
Building My World	
Sorting Our World	page83.pdf
Back in Time	page88.pdf
New York Stories	page94.pdf
A Path Through History	page100.pdf
Language Arts	
Customizing Placemarks	page106.pdf
Jack's Journey	page112.pdf
Take Me There	page118.pdf
Telling a Story	page124.pdf

Contents of Teacher Resource CD *(cont.)*

Social Studies	
Times Will Change	page130.pdf
Magellan's Journey	page136.pdf
Then and Now	page142.pdf
Earthquake Strikes!	page149.pdf
Science	
Runoff Through the Great Lakes	page154.pdf
Destructive Volcanoes	page161.pdf
Night and Day	page166.pdf
Fuel Sources	page173.pdf
Mathematics	
Washington, DC	page178.pdf
Subtracting the Amazon	page184.pdf
Plots of Land	page190.pdf
Water All Around	page196.pdf
Beyond Earth	
To the Moon	page203.pdf
How Deep Is the Ocean?	page209.pdf
Where in the World...?	page214.pdf
Ancient Drawings	page220.pdf

Notes

Notes

Notes

Notes

Notes